My Resurrection from Hell

Tales of a Christian Widower

*To Norma,
thank you for
being there
Lewis Tagliaferre*

LEWIS TAGLIAFERRE

ISBN 978-1-0980-0067-7 (paperback)
ISBN 978-1-0980-0068-4 (digital)

Copyright © 2019 by Lewis Tagliaferre

All rights reserved. No part of this publication may be reproduced, distributed, or transmitted in any form or by any means, including photocopying, recording, or other electronic or mechanical methods without the prior written permission of the publisher. For permission requests, solicit the publisher via the address below.

Christian Faith Publishing, Inc.
832 Park Avenue
Meadville, PA 16335
www.christianfaithpublishing.com

Printed in the United States of America

DISCLAIMER

There are many secular challenges facing people who lose control of their lives through aging, death, and other human disasters. The American Psychological Association (APA) convened a study group to define the issues people in distress must cope with. They are beyond the scope of this book, but I am listing them here with the instruction to seek professional help from qualified counselors if these problems are beyond your ability to manage them alone. If the discussion in this book makes you feel scared and confused, that could be normal because all growth requires suffering. But if you feel depressed and have uncontrollable anxiety, please seek professional care immediately. Nothing in this book is intended to be a substitute for competent medical or mental health diagnosis and treatment.

Mental health concerns
Depression
Anxiety
Guilt, sadness, dread, worry
Suicide prevention

Physical health concerns
Fatigue
Sleep problems
Illness, injury, mortality
Medical treatment
Diet

Functional impairment
Fall proofing the dwelling
Daily in-home support
Personal transportation
Cleaning and housekeeping
Food arrangements

Secondary strains
Work—employment
Financial strains
Relationship stress
Time management

Lifestyle decisions
Social activities
Residential options
Recreation events
End of life planning

Government resources
Housing
Healthcare
Community services
Respite Care
Disability Insurance
Social Security benefits

Family challenges
Conflict about care
Lack of support for caregiver
Balancing needs family members
Behavioral issues
Interpersonal conflicts

Advocacy for care
Compliance by care recipient
Interface with service systems
Coordinating various providers
Legal assignment for care providers

www.apa.org

CONTENTS

Acknowledgments 7
Prologue 9

Part I. In the Beginning..11
    My Family of Origin 13
    The Growing Up Years 26

Part II. Maturity and Beyond 47
    The Years at NECA 49
    Loving and Losing...75

Part III. Lessons Learned 93
    Mindful Living...95
    Emotions Regulation...107
    Distress Tolerance..124
    Interpersonal Communications 139

Part IV. Resurrection from Hell 147
    Growing Beyond the Bible 149
    My New Revelation..158

Epilogue 173
Appendix A 175
Appendix B 180

ACKNOWLEDGMENTS

I am thankful to Adam Mellott and his team at Christian Faith Publishing for making this book possible. I also am thankful for the many published resources that I was given throughout the years in which I was struggling to survive. There is no way I could have found them without some divine intervention that drove me to seek a way out of hell. The professional counselors and therapists who showed amazing persistence and tenacity when I resisted their attempts to change my thinking also are greatly appreciated. I also thank all those people in my life who tolerated my incessant needs to repeat my lamentations endlessly. I especially thank my son who never let me go and always was a steady hand in my deepest sorrow. I thank whatever gods may be for my unconquerable soul. If you find this work helpful, I thank you for referring it to others who may need to be resurrected from hell.

PROLOGUE

My life ended and a new one began at 7:20 p.m. on September 3, 1985, in room 232 of the Arlington Hospital. That is where I held her right hand with my left one and watched my wife, Rosalene (her real name), die untimely at her age of fifty-two. I always loved to hold her hand. As she exhaled for the last time, I told her Jesus and her mother and father would be there waiting for her. I told her I and our kids would be okay so she could let go without worrying about us. What a fool I was. She looked up to the right at the clock on the wall as if to note the time of her death and then exhaled softly and sank into the pillow. One eye closed partially, but the other one remained open. I placed my left hand over her eyes and lightly closed them. Her eyelids moved down without any resistance over her sightless eyes, and I knew the life, whatever that is, had left her body. The nurse who was standing by the foot of the bed said, "Wasn't that beautiful?"

The nurses removed all the attachments and machines from the room. They left the body of Rosalene lying in repose that evening so her brother and sister-in-law and my two children and I could spend the last hours in her presence. At 11:00 p.m., we left her body there in the bed, and I never saw her again. As we left the room, I tweaked her exposed toe, which had turned blue and cold, sticking out from the cover and said, "Good-bye, Rosalene." She always slept with one foot uncovered. Her body was removed to the hospital morgue and transferred to the mortuary we had selected the next morning. That night, I and the kids slept fitfully together on the floor in the living room. Her brother and his wife took me to the mortuary the next morning to make final plans, but I could not leave the car. So, they made the arrangements, which included identifying the body. They also informed the church office of her passing. We had made plans for cremation, so the church arranged for a gathering at the funeral home on Friday evening.

On the drive to the hospital that last time, I cried and asked her, "How in the world can I continue working without you until I can retire?" She replied, "Oh, by then, you will have forgotten all about these times." You can tell I have not forgotten. They say that widowers either die or get married again. I have done neither. I have learned a lot about myself, experienced the process of grieving the most stressful of all losses, and survived in a form of new life I could never have imagined. The founder of dialectical behavior therapy, Dr. Marsha Linehan (1943–), said we must suffer misery to get out of hell.

This memoir is the story of my journey through loss and the resurrection from hell that has brought me to this place in a life that I did not think was worth living any longer. Here you will find a history of my life and details of our marriage and what happened to me after she was gone. Many people expect widowers to go on as though nothing happened. But something great happened, and I wanted the world to stop and pay attention. I don't know why I have lived this long, unless it is to learn how to survive this greatest of losses and to share what I learned through the books I have been given to write. This is my story. It might help you live yours.

Note: Except for my immediate family, the names of people included in this memoir all are disguised to protect their privacy, but the situations are real just as I remember them.

PART I

In the Beginning

In this first part, I lay the foundation for the life I was given. Every life begins someplace sometime. Even though we may not realize it, we are influenced by the family and social circumstances in which we are born. Most of us do the best we can under the circumstances. None of us can go back in time to do anything differently no matter how much we may want to. Swiss psychiatrist, C. G. Jung (1875–1960), said, "Your pathway is not my pathway. Therefore, I cannot teach you. The pathway is within." The symbol I have chosen for this work is the ancient labyrinth inlaid in the floor of the Chartres Cathedral of France. Unlike a random maze that is designed to frustrate and confuse, the labyrinth presents a walk of life one cannot avoid. We leave the source in the center at birth to walk through the four quadrants of infancy, childhood, youth, and adulthood. Then after midlife, we return to the source through quadrants of maturity, seniority, contemplation, and mortality. Whatever your belief may be, we all must walk the pathway we are given. This is the story of my life as I remember it.

My Family of Origin

I was born on January 31, 1933, at 4:00 a.m. during a snowstorm in a house no longer existing at 10 Jones Street in Ridgeley, West Virginia, according to my mother. My father was Raffaele Tagliaferri, and my mother was Anna Marie Maier. He was born on September 14, 1890, in the village of Marigliano near Naples, Italy. She was born on February 7, 1895, in the town of Patterson's Creek, West Virginia. They were married in 1913 and survived the flu epidemic of 1918. When I was born, my father was age forth-three, and my mother was age thirty-eight. I was not their first kid. My father said they conceived a son before me who was born dead, so they buried him without a birth certificate. Hence, they were always worried about my safety and always tried to keep me out of harm's way, sometimes overdoing it in my opinion. Although they never said so, I believe that they loved me.

I know little of my father's youth except the brief verbal history that I recall from his limited and rare conversations about it. The only record I have is his birth certificate. His father was listed as Guiseppe Tagliaferri, and his mother as Antoinetta Panico. I seem to recall that he had a stepmother so his mother may have died during his childhood. He described his family as peasant farmers who sold their produce in a street market in Naples, which required leaving the house very early to make the trek by ox cart during the season. Their house had an earthen floor, which they shared with various goats and chickens. There was a sleeping loft above the floor reached by a wooden ladder. There was no inside plumbing or stove. Refrigeration was unheard of as possibly also was electricity. The backyard had a dung heap, which they shared with the animals. He recalled the mild climate and the profusion of lemons that still are known for that region. It is located within the shadow of Mt. Vesuvius, which you may recall erupted in AD 79 covering the villages of Pompeii and

Herculaneum. He had a brother and sister at least as he wrote and got letters from them. He commented that his father was very brutal and often beat his wife with a coiled-up rope. At one point, a man was found shot dead in their cornfield, and although his father was investigated, nothing further came of it.

Somehow, my grandfather obtained a patronage contract to work for three years in US coal mines at Thomas, West Virginia. Sometime after his departure, he arranged for my father, who was the eldest child, to make the same journey at the age of fourteen, under the supervision of some traveling guardian. He described the trip as very long and scary and being utterly seasick for more than a week at sea, on the coal-fired steamship, the *Italia*. It was built for the Anchor Line specifically to bring immigrants to America and was scrapped in 1925. It was a single stack vessel rated at 2,451 tons with capacity of a hundred first class state rooms that were "well ventilated" on deck and seven hundred steerage bunks below. The salon was equipped with a piano, library, and "other luxuries." I obtained the shipping manifest with his name on the list. She arrived in dock at New York on November 30, 1904.

When he arrived at Ellis Island in New York, he was tagged like a piece of luggage, given a sack lunch, and put onto a train that took him to Thomas, West Virginia, where his father was waiting for him. They worked together in the coal mines under gaslights while living in a boxcar with other immigrant miners. It must have been a very rugged way of life. At the age of seventeen, his father returned to Italy, but he was able to remain somehow and obtained work on the construction crews building the B&O Railroad through the mountains on its way to Ohio. First, he was a "water boy" searching out springs for the crews to drink, and later, he graduated to laying the track. He was only five feet six inches, but he was burly and claimed that he could carry a full section of track on his shoulder alone. At some time, he attended a funeral in Cumberland, Maryland, of a worker killed in an accident, and there he met my mother. I never recall getting any details of their first encounter. By that time, he must have learned enough English to get by and decided to stay in the US to avoid military service in Italy if he returned. He never visited his homeland again, although he did keep up by letters with some of his siblings. I don't know when, but I believe he became a US citizen.

Now for the other side of my ancestors. My mother said that her family emigrated to the US from Essen, Germany. She was one of seven children, being the first to be born in the US. Her siblings in order were Louis, Elizabeth, Mary, Engelbert, Kate, herself, and George the youngest. I don't know what work her father did or the names of her parents, except her maiden name was Anna Marie Maier; she was called Annie. I know nothing of her childhood except she said her father was often brutal with the boys when they misbehaved. She was spoiled between her elder sister, my aunt Kate, and her younger brother, Uncle George, as might be expected. I have never wanted to visit the homelands of either parent. I can tour them sufficiently on Google Earth.

According to my mother, Aunt Elizabeth (Lizzie) attended my birth about 4:00 a.m. as midwife at 10 Jones Street in Ridgeley, West Virginia, just across the Potomac River from Cumberland. Since it was snowing, the doctor did not get there until daybreak and immediately took me and my mother to the hospital where she was sedated. When he filled out my birth certificate, my father spelled my name wrong because my mother said I was to be named Louis Robert for her oldest brother. In the confusion, my father wrote out Lewis Tagliaferre, so that is how I got my name. My mother was very upset, but they never attempted to get it corrected. I don't think they knew that they could.

My mother claimed her life was very hard growing up. She was taken out of school at age twelve and put to work at a silk mill in Cumberland, Maryland. She had to walk the several miles for a twelve-hour workday, and during the harsh winters, she said sometimes the snow came up to her knees. She must have been a beautiful young woman because she was blonde and blue-eyed and weighed about 118 pounds when she got married in 1913. She claimed that she had a boyfriend who was not a Catholic named Lawrence Bach whom her father rejected. When she met my father who was

Catholic, she was pushed into getting married and chose that alternative to avoid the harsh life at the mill.

They bought the house at 10 Jones Street—demolished and replaced—and settled into marriage while my father obtained work at the Kelly-Springfield tire plant across the Potomac River in Cumberland. He worked there during the Great Depression until the start of WWII. She said that he took a shortcut to work by rowing across the river in a boat he kept moored nearby and skated across in the winter when the river was frozen over. She said he had a fierce temper when they got married and liked to drink beer, consuming a case on the weekends and cursing God when things went wrong. However, he was invited by a coworker to attend a tent revival meeting three years after they married, and there he became a converted member of the Assemblies of God church. After that, he hated Catholics and so alienated all my mother's relatives such that a few of them ever visited us. My mother attended church with him, but she never gave up her Catholic tradition and often prayed her rosary. She was able to walk to visit her elder sister, Kate, nearby.

I have only vague memories of the house in Ridgeley, West Virginia. I recall riding my trike around the rooms inside and a grill in the floor that let heat from the coal furnace in the basement rise through the floor to upstairs. I have no recollection of the kitchen or the bathroom. I remember eating "chicken legs" my mother made by rolling ground meat onto a sucker stick and frying it in lard. For snacks, she just fried flour into a pancake or served sugared bread soaked in warm milk. She was not getting pregnant, so they took in the infant son of some distant relative of my father from Brooklyn, New York, to help out temporarily in 1920. The mother died and the father became deaf, so they ended up keeping him although without formal adoption. They named him Paul. He was thirteen years old when I was born. Then in 1935, they had my younger brother they named George William after Uncle George.

In 1938, they moved to a twelve-acre tract into a small two-bedroom brick house that my father built with the help of some friends in the developing area called Bowman's Addition, three miles outside of Cumberland in one of the several valleys of that mountainous area. The valley runs north-south so the sun comes up late and sets early. This was a major change for my mother because it removed her from the walkable nearness of relatives in Ridgeley, and it isolated her from shopping in the downtown center on Baltimore Street. She became a very obese recluse by age forty-three and from then, she never left the house, but she got up early to fire up the coal furnace in winter and make breakfast to get my brother and me off to school. She never ate with the rest of us because she had few teeth, and I presumed she was embarrassed. I never knew how she spent the day alone, but she did the washing, ironing, and cooking. She also made her own dresses and aprons from chicken feed sacks with the foot treadle Singer sewing machine, and she always walked around in soft bedroom slippers.

After we moved, the only relatives who kept in touch were Aunt Kate and Uncle George. Kate was married to Russell Smith with two daughters, Ruth Ella and Agnes. Ruth Ella married Bill Barr, and Agnes married Roy Ritchie and both lived in Ridgeley, West Virginia, near their parents. Uncle George never married and was an itinerate worker on a local dairy farm. Uncle Louis died tragically shortly before his planned retirement in a railroad accident when he fell off a boxcar working as a brakeman. My father took me to their house where the body was laid out in the living room. His wife was screaming and lurching over the half-open casket because his lower body was missing. Two boxcars had cut him in half at the waistline, crushing his watch. They did not have any children. Uncle Engelbert died of a heart attack when I was very young. He was married to Aunt Margaret, and they had nine kids. There were some other cousins much older than I, but they rarely visited us, so I have no connections with that side of the family. I recall a mail correspondence later in high school with a cousin in Italy named Mary. After I got married, she asked if I would sponsor her immigration to America, but Rosalene said no way. I lost touch with her, so I have no connections with any relatives in the homeland of my father.

My mother refused to attend church with my father and held onto her Catholic faith, praying the rosary for the rest of her life. There was constant friction as she wanted him to visit the St. Peter and Paul Cathedral at least on high holy days, but he never would. After I began to attend school in 1939, she never ever attended any events or took interest in my school life, except to sign my report cards. My father came to parent-teacher events, but she never did. I think she became clinically depressed and probably suffered greatly until she died in Memorial Hospital of a massive stroke at age sixty-five in December 1960 without regaining consciousness. During the final viewing before they closed the casket, my father cried and said, "My god, I loved that woman." I really know that feeling. He said he really liked her nose. Whenever I visited him, he wanted me to sit on his lap and often asked me if I loved him. Although I said yes, I really did not like him very much. I felt little remorse after leaving them at age eighteen, but later, it set in, and I was sorry for the suffering that my mother must have endured on my account.

My father continued his work at Kelly-Springfield throughout the Depression years, but he had to return to the B&O Railroad in 1940 when the tire plant was converted to making ammunition for the WWII war effort. He worked at the Bolt and Forge shop in Cumberland, managed by the late Roy Everson who later was the mayor of Cumberland. He remained there until he retired, but he could not obtain daywork and worked second shift from 3:00 p.m. to 11:00 p.m. all during my high school years, repairing and testing pneumatic air brake valves after running a hydraulic punch press that shaped sheet metal for boxcar repairs. I only saw him on weekends. He would leave instructions with my mother for chores in the garden and yard, which I never complained about, while my brother got to play. I learned to be dependable, and he learned to play. After I left home to join the Air Force, the housecleaning suffered because he did not take up my chores. When I returned on leave, there were cobwebs on the curtains.

I attended grade school at the Columbia Street School. Paul drove me and a neighbor named Frank Cook on the first day in 1939. The first-grade teacher was nice, but I feared Miss Higgins, the principal. I liked school from the beginning and still enjoy learning. The school had no cafeteria, so I took sandwiches from home. By the fourth grade, I began to sense something was different about my family by the way I was dressed compared to other kids. In the sixth grade, I was appointed captain of the safety patrols, and, with my lieutenant, Wayne Miller, I walked the beat checking up on the rank and file. I transferred for seventh grade to Fort Hill High School. My bus ride was the first round on two trips, so we had to stand outside, sometimes in bad weather, until the school was opened. I recall getting on the bus in winter with snow up to the bus hubcaps. I concentrated on my schoolwork and developed a pseudo extraverted personality that belied the real world at home. For example, during the fall, my father would go to slaughterhouses and take home the rejected parts of hogs that we ate. We also raised chickens, ducks, and rabbits, which were butchered on Saturday mornings. If I had to kill animals to eat meat, I would be a vegetarian. You have not lived if you have never seen a chicken with its head cut off and smelled it doused in boiling water to pluck the feathers or dodged the blood from a headless rabbit hung upside down being skinned. I never entertained other kids at home because I was ashamed of the way we lived and kept to myself at school. I was dressed like a country hillbilly and shied away from any public exposure. There was a bathroom with a tub, but I don't recall ever taking a bath…strange. From Thanksgiving until Easter, we wore whole-body long underwear, which sometimes was exposed to view—a total embarrassment to me. I wore flannel shirts, blue jeans, and "clodhopper" brogan shoes. Nevertheless, I must have exhibited some intelligence as several teachers gave me some special encouragement, and I always earned good grades. In my school yearbook, one teacher wrote, "Remember us when you become a senator."

    We had no tree at Christmas, so I sometimes cut some pine boughs to drape over the door lintels. Birthdays were just another day. My mother would say, "Well, Lewis, you are a year older now." Toys were a pure luxury, so we made our own. Although we had some metal cars and trucks, and we did get a used bicycle that had to be shared, we made most toys for ourselves. I recall making a rubber-band gun from tire inner tubes wrapped around a piece of wood, making a bow and arrow set from wild bamboo and dried stalks, creating a dart from corn cobs stuffed with a nail and chicken feathers that we threw at rain barrels, and sliding down the hill on a sled made of scrap wood during the cold harsh winters. One time, a kid from school named Norman McDonald sailed a homemade dart over top of the rain barrel and broke the kitchen window where my father was sitting at the table. The kid ran home and never came back. I made a rather accurate wooden replica of a rifle that my father broke in two over his knee as punishment for something I don't remember.

I was not allowed to play athletic games with neighbors because my mother was afraid that I would get hurt, and the few times I disobeyed, she was right. Once during a field football game, I sprained my right ankle badly. If we got sick or hurt, there were just home remedies and rarely a visit from the doctor, who made home calls. There was a neighbor boy named Donnie Davis who would challenge me to a game of checkers. Usually, he lost, but he kept coming back. I remember having crushes on two neighbor girls. One was cute, and one had a bad scar on her hand. I remember trading Marvel comic books with other kids. We had to use our imagination on the action comics. I recall Dick Tracy, Superman, Flash Gordon, and Batman. Now, I see action movies as very expensive comic books. There were no library books to read except the ones in school. I remember reading one titled *Black Beauty* about a horse and one about a dog. I recall playing marbles, but I was not very good at it. There was a game where we cut a round hole in a match box and dropped marbles into it from your waistline. If it went in, you got to choose a marble and if it didn't, you lost yours.

My brother was very militant and liked to argue and pick fights with me. I was usually able to pin him down. He also was masochistic with the animals. One time, he took a kitten up on the back roof and dropped it off to see if it would land on its feet. I threw a stone at a duck once and hit it in the head, killing it. My mother butchered it right away, but I did not get punished. I really don't have many memories of what we did during the long summer vacations. One thing I recall was making pencil drawings on a sketch pad. I was pretty good at it. I recall scary thunder and lightning storms. My mother said that thunder was God rolling rain barrels around in heaven. I would stand in the open front door watching sheets of rain roll up the valley. After the storms passed, the air would be cooler for a while until the humid heat returned in full force.

Paul was thirteen years older, so he was not much involved in my life. However, at the age of seventeen, he learned somehow that my parents were not his real father and mother, which caused a severe rift and a lot of yelling and screaming. He dropped out of high school and was taken in by some church family named Maviston. He also was converted to the Assemblies of God faith, same as my father, which my mother hated. The subsequent disruption caused a great deal of arguing between my parents, but they reconciled, and he returned after a couple years and managed to finish high school at age twenty. He left immediately and got married later and moved to Pittsburgh, so he played no further role in my life. My younger brother, George, was much different than I so we drifted apart after puberty and had little in common the rest of our lives. He was married three times and lost the land in his first divorce, the house in the second, and ended up living in a trailer park after the third. He died at age seventy-one from complications of surgery for a ruptured aorta in January 2006.

There was no telephone and only a radio and a manual crank-up RCA Victrola phonograph player with a collection of records my mother had saved. We used an ice box, and my job was to carry out the drip water. Water flowed slowly down the hill from a spring. It was very "hard," meaning full of minerals, which tasted awful. I still don't like to drink water. We collected "soft" rainwater from the down spouts in barrels for washing dishes and clothing. It was a big deal when my mother got an electric Maytag washing machine after scrubbing clothes by hand. She hung them up on a clothesline in the backyard. After they dried, she would have to shake soot off from the locomotives in town that drifted our way. There were no soft drinks, other than homemade lemonade in summers. Milk was delivered by a farmer nearby, and in winter, I would skim cream off the top that popped out from the cold. I still love cream. My mother cooked on a combination of wood and coal stove that I had to keep stocked with kindling wood cut from slabs discarded by a sawmill my father picked up free of charge in his Model T Ford truck. I recall helping her can vegetables from the garden while sweating over the stove in the summer heat. The house was heated by a coal furnace that produced so much soot all the walls had to be washed down each spring. My father cut the weeds around the house with a scythe. When I was about age ten, I was attacked by a swarm of hornets I dislodged while raking some grass. I just sat down and screamed until my father came running to rescue me. The pain was acute as I had many stings, including in my nose, ears, and mouth.

We were not allowed to attend movies or any school parties. I was even prevented from engaging in folk dancing in second grade with a note from home. I was excused by Miss Hamill to stand aside during that class period, which only made me more conspicuous and embarrassed. For some reason, my mother dressed me up and sent me off to Sunday school and church with my father for several years. I still wonder why she did that because she never included my brother. One man scared me by jumping up in the middle of the sermon speaking in tongues almost every Sunday. I felt pressured to make a commitment of faith, but I never did because I reasoned that since religion caused such trouble between my parents, I would join whatever faith my future wife might have for the sake of family unity. While my father was engaged in the post service "alter call," I would wait in the car. I could hear wailing coming through the open windows in the summer. It seems ironic, but after the church relocated to Bedford Road, the old building was converted into a performing arts theater. I am sure my father would not approve.

My father gave me the impression that all normal entertainment is a mortal sin to be avoided at all costs. Even going to the annual county fair was prohibited. Entertainment of any kind was out of the question. It was odd that he let me play trumpet in a dance band. He absolutely panicked when he learned that I and two friends were learning some dance steps from a neighbor girl pending the senior prom, which I did not attend. Neither did I get a class ring. I did not get to date in high school, although I did have a special friendship with one neighbor girl, Jean Akers, who would ride her bike to my house and chat with my mother. Mom said she was glad she never had a girl because the child would have had a miserable life. Jean got married right after graduation to an older man. I did not feel the loss acutely because I enlisted and left home. But I never forgot her. When I visited her on my first leave from the Air Force, she would not invite me in, but she hugged me and said, "Oh, Lewy, I should have waited for you." I called her after Rosalene died with my lamentation, and she said that God may have taken Rosalene to remove an idol that I allowed to stand between him and me. I could understand that, but it did not make me feel happy about God.

My father had somehow learned to play the piano a little and the cornet, so we had one of each. Around the fourth grade, he started me on the cornet and by the time I entered middle school, I was good enough, mostly self-taught, to play in the band. Later, my mother gave me $180 cash to buy a new Conn trumpet, and nobody could figure out where she got that much money. We would sit around making music at home, including my attempts to sing and play the acoustic guitar, which my mother also bought for me, along with a do-it-yourself instruction book from Doc Williams who performed on the radio from Wheeling, West Virginia. Mostly, we sang hymns and country folk songs. Dad (I never really knew what to call him) let me play in a professional dance band around town that was conducted by a man named Rudy Sully—and his Ambassadors—at the local civic club parties and dinner dances and such. Those gigs provided the money for my personal needs. I saw enough drinking and rowdy behavior among women and men that shaped my values away from them. I never would play in his church, and I think that disappointed him greatly. When I came home from a gig on school nights, he kept me awake reading Bible stories to me. He would say, "You have been out there, so now listen to this."

The Conn trumpet I was able to buy with money hoarded by my mother eventually made me into a minor local celebrity. It was my door into social society at school, but I was too embarrassed to have school chums visit my poor home and see my living conditions. I became a loner to protect my self-esteem and remained so all my life. Even in the Air Force barracks with eighty men, I remained alone on my bunk or took walks to hide. The money I earned playing at dances came in handy for clothing and extra school activities. I took the driver training class in school and soon as I reached age sixteen, my father got my driving license. He let me drive our 1932 Chevrolet to the football games. After I put a big dent in the back corner while backing into a parked truck, he let me paint the whole thing robin's egg blue with yellow spoke wheels. With a brush. Amazing. Changing a frequently flat tire was a manly chore, requiring much effort to pump up the inner tube with a manual pump. So was changing spark plugs and making carburetor and timing adjustments. The car had mechanical brakes, which required a lot of push to stop the thing. I broke the rear axle trying to climb a steep street by popping it into low gear, but he did not punish me. I never really saw him lose his temper or become violent.

My father would not assent to my attending college, although Frostburg State, only twelve miles away, offered free tuition for teacher trainees. So, I bypassed the college-prep program and took the general curriculum because he told me to get all I could out of high school. A businessman and mortician offered to grant me a scholarship through the University of Maryland, but my father refused. I probably would not be admitted anyway because I did not take the college-prep courses. Their plan was for me to stay home after I graduated and work until age twenty-one, repaying them for raising me. My mother thought I should become a barber because people will always need their hair cut. My father's ambition for me was the machinist apprentice program on the railroad. I took the test, but they said I failed it. I think they rejected me because my father was a vocal critic of the union. They restricted productivity by imposing piece-rate rules on his job. He arranged for me to work at the railroad shops on two summer vacations, and I worked in a shoe store during a winter vacation. I got a $1 bonus for selling the most shoes in one day, mostly to women.

I supplemented the academic subjects in high school with balanced classes in public speaking, typing, vocational arts, and drama, starring in two stage productions under the drama coach, Miss Smythe. One was as father in *Life with Mother*, and the other was a pipe-smoking detective in the murder mystery, *Drums of Death*. I also won a speech contest on the United Nations, which involved a trip to New York City during my senior year. It was on the trip that I met Miss Rosalene M. Dettra, who had won for Bruce High School in Westernport, Maryland. She would later become my wife. She was not much impressed with me at first because I was from the stuck-up high school, and I was the lead trumpet player in the all-county band concert.

The highlights of my school memories include the band marching for football games and the parades during special holidays and special concerts. I was the student conductor and directed the pep band at rallies and basketball games. We were selected to escort the Maryland Lions club to its national convention in New York where I got to conduct the dance ensemble in Madison Square Garden, and we marched down Constitution Avenue in Washington DC, escorting the school patrol club of Maryland. By the time I graduated in 1951, the Korean War was on, and young men my age were getting drafted. So, a drummer friend from the high school band, Tom Elsworth, and I decided to enlist in the US Air Force to avoid the army infantry. We waited until the fall to avoid basic training in the hot summer heat of Texas, so I got a job as the stock clerk in the Cumberland Cloak and Suit store that summer. That was my first experience handling women's clothing, especially underwear. I also learned about retail markups.

They could hold a half-price sale and still make money. Then came the first great shock of my life.

The Growing Up Years

Let's face it, I was a fat kid. I skipped gym class in school to avoid being embarrassed and harassed. The coaches gave me a "satisfactory" on my report cards anyway. I was also bullied in fourth grade by an older redheaded kid in sixth grade named Paul Gother. He would crush my hand in a "friendly shake," and once, he forced me to put my tongue on a cold metal post in winter that caused a big scar when I pulled it off. Kids used to call me "dago, honky, wop, and lard butt." When I told my mother, she just gave me a phrase to recite as follows: "Sticks and stones can break my bones, but words can never hurt me." During the winter vacation in my senior year, I was very sick with a serious flu and lost several pounds. I was about five feet ten inches tall and weighed about 170 pounds when I enlisted in the US Air Force in September after graduation. My mother took my departure very hard and hugged me fiercely the day we left. At first, she claimed, "They won't take you because you are not like those other boys." I had to find out if she was right. The day I left, she wept and wailed, "Don't go, Lewis, don't leave me." I recall spending some quality talks with her when I was at home sick a few times. That is when she would tell me about her youth and early marriage years. When I realized she had sex with my father to conceive me, I lost some respect for her and so was ready to leave for my own shot at the world. One time, she said, "He has trampled my love under my feet so many times there is none left." I told her, "You have had your life. Now it is time for me to have mine." Little did I know what was in store.

The bedrooms had no doors, only curtains, and I recall sometimes hearing my father getting off. After I realized what was happening, it disgusted me. They call it the "primal scream" when kids realize that their parents are hooking up. However, the lack of doors was useful because if I could not go to sleep, I called for my mother,

"Mom, I can't go to sleep," and she called back, "Just say the Lord's Prayer three times and you will go to sleep." It usually worked; in the Air Force, too. So, the bedrooms without doors came with benefits as well as burdens. That is life. I felt apprehensive about leaving to face the ultimate uncertainty, but something inside me pushed me on just to see if I could make it. I still feel some remorse for leaving her, but the army beckoned, and by the end of my Air Force service, I was married. I think she was depressed at my loss until she died.

My father was always calm and never lost his temper even when I broke a tool or did something foolish. However, I had the impression that I better obey as ordered or something terrible would happen to me, although it never did. So, living under military rules did not bother me after I got used to it. When I left, he said, "Write to us sometimes."

We were bused to the induction center in Martinsburg, West Virginia. After we were stripped and examined, I swore allegiance to the US Constitution and agreed to obey orders. It was embarrassing to say the least because I had never been naked before in person. Then came a sleepless overnight train ride to the basic training center on Lake Seneca near Geneva in New York state named Sampson Air Force Base. The base in Texas had become overloaded with recruits, and Sampson was activated to expand basic military training. It was a beautiful location on a lake such as I had never seen before. We arrived at daybreak on September 29, 1951, and then were bused to the base about ten miles south. As we collected our luggage at the train terminal, I recall some graduating recruits who were leaving for their training assignments heckled us with jeers about what we faced. We spent a lot of the first day waiting in lines to fill out forms and get haircuts and issued clothing, shots, always escorted by our assigned training instructor or TI. After my first breakfast, I got sick to my stomach and vomited in the street. I wondered what I had gotten into and whether I could survive four years.

That evening, we got assigned to bunks in our barracks, and the TI showed us how to make up the bedding to inspection order. He put us to bed with this warning, "We can't make you do anything, but we sure as hell can make you wish you had." The next morning at 4:30 a.m., all hell broke loose when we were rudely awakened by a shrill whistle, and it just continued that way for ten weeks. I don't recall his name, but he was a total disaster as a leader, and we fell way behind in training. He was replaced in about two weeks by a much better TI. His name was Corporal Blander. He was awaiting departure for the new Air Force Academy and would be our mother of all things for our basic training. I took an upper bunk, and Tom took the lower. There were forty of us in the "flight" as we were called. Double bunks were arranged in order with ten on each side in two-story sparse wooden WWII barracks. We were instructed to write a note home saying we had arrived okay and were in good spirits, something we had to do each Friday evening. I recall it got so cold in those barracks later in the fall that the water in cigarette butt cans nailed to the posts was frozen in the mornings. They had civilians stoking the coal-fired furnaces during the day, but they left after the dayshift and let the fire die out at night. Go figure.

Corporal Blander was in our faces all the time, except for when he was spelled by the drill sergeant or some classroom instructor. We had to learn quickly how to use the latrine (bathroom) and SSS—shit, shave, and shower—and get dressed and ready for reveille in less than an hour. There was no place for privacy, and modesty was out of the question. In the latrine, there were ten or twelve sinks with mirrors for shaving, a line of open commodes, a communal urinal, and a large open bay shower room. There I learned how to be alone in the middle of a crowd. The mass confusion that existed those first days was unimaginable. But we soon got into the routine and would "fall in" outside the barracks from the tallest to the shortest, and then be marched to the chow hall for breakfast. Food in my home was barely adequate with lots of fresh garden produce in season and mostly canned food in the winter and freshly butchered meat. My mother specialized in deep dish pizza, home baked bread, and spaghetti. She made her own sauce and grew fresh basil. While a few guys complained about the chow I never did, and I always took seriously the banner over the serving line that said, "Take all you want, eat all you take." Food was served cafeteria style on heavy metal trays. To this day, I have the compulsion to clean up my plate.

MY RESURRECTION FROM HELL

    I took the regimentation in stride, but one of our flight recruits had to be released as unfit because he just could not obey the rules and was disorderly and defiant. Except for a few minor screwups, I got through basic in good shape, better than I had ever been, at only 155 pounds. One time, when I screwed up in drill, the TI yelled at me, "Airman, I am going to cut a hole in your stomach so we can see your head when it is up your ass." My mother wrote a letter to the TI asking them to take care of me. I was called into the office by Corporal Blander and ordered to tell her that I was not being abused. I guess it depends on your perception. I got terribly painful oozing foot blisters during close order drill in brogans that were too tight. I went on sick call where the medic splashed them with iodine and stuck on adhesive tape. I still remember the pain. They eventually healed as the shoes broke in, and I passed all the physical and classroom requirements, including the firing range and the final obstacle course. But I never wore the spare brogans or dress shoes during my entire enlistment. And it never occurred to me to buy replacements of a larger size.

    One time, Tom made some wise cracks to a classroom instructor, and the whole flight was punished with extra drill. That night, they gave us both a "blanket party," but there were no broken bones, so we survived. I recall falling asleep in the overheated barracks as we sat on the floor to hear the Uniform Code of Military Justice read to us by several different readers. It took all day. I began to realize how much freedom we lost to protect the country from the advancement of communism. We had three days of testing to see what career field to select, and after it became obvious that they did not need any trumpet players, I was assigned to electronics and ground radar school at Keesler AFB, Mississippi. Tom was assigned to a different school at the same base. I would have preferred control tower operator, but my faulty depth perception ruled that out. We were flown down to Biloxi, Mississippi, on December 10, 1951. Did I say they did not need trumpet players? Losing my horn was the first loss I never properly grieved.

    The climate shock was severe, leaving the cloudy winter temps in New York for the sunny tropics on the Gulf Coast. The walkways were covered with crushed seashells, making the sunlit brightness almost unbearable. I recall it took a day for processing. I was miserable and sweating, dressed in the winter blue uniform. The summer khakis were not much better, and we sweated practically all the time. School began immediately, and the pressure for discipline was relaxed somewhat, although we marched to classes and had supervised study for three hours each evening after a full six-hour day in class and lab. They just would not let you fail. When I returned home for a week of leave at Christmas by train, my mother hardly recognized me and almost refused to believe it was I, myself. She looked at me and lamented, "You're not Lewis. You don't even look like Lewis." I suppose I had changed considerably, and my appearance in the blue uniform must have been a shock to her. Again, there was much wailing when I left. She wanted me to stay home even if she had to hide me in the attic. I rarely got a letter from my father because he barely wrote legible English, and none from my brother. But my mother wrote weekly long letters written in pencil on lined notepaper, spilling out her grief and depression over my departure. I never saved any of them. I wish I had. I have only one letter from my father several years later, which I framed.

I completed the six-month electronics school without special incident. Possibly our dumbest stunt was driving home on a three-day pass over the President's Day weekend in February, which was illegal. Tom had to replace the cracked head on his 1940 Chevy, and we barely made it back in time for school on Monday evening. Another hour or so later and we could have been court-martialed. I don't think we slept for three days. Next came three more months of specialized training on the specific ground radar equipment I was assigned to service. After that, my buddy was shipped off to Korea, so we lost touch.

A civilian instructor, Mr. Hobart, took a liking to me and arranged for me to be retained as a full-time instructor upon graduation, which included three months more of train-the-trainer class. This was almost unheard of as the instructors all had field experience before returning for classroom duty. It also meant quick promotions for me as soon as the required time in grade passed. I lectured for three hours per day and supervised lab for three hours followed by three hours of lesson preparation. I had plenty of free time to spend lounging on the Biloxi beach where I would prepare my lesson plans. This was to prove problematic when I developed a form of basal cell skin cancer much later from all that sunbathing.

I must backtrack for something very important. When I returned home for leave during the summer of 1952 for some reason, my father took me with him to a funeral being conducted in Westernport, Maryland. I recalled that Rosalene Dettra, who I met on the high school senior trip to NYC, lived there. While he attended the funeral, I drove to the church manse where her father was pastor of the local Church of the Brethren to visit her unannounced. She was not home, being at a church summer camp, but I chatted with her mother and father. They seemed to be so much different than my own parents that I immediately felt a desire to model my life after them. I must have made an impression because after I returned to base, Rosalene started up a pen pal writing campaign, which was not unusual for girls writing to GIs at that time. When I returned the next Christmas season, I did get to visit with her at home while she was on college break. I distinctly recall a good-bye kiss—after I asked, of course—that instantly cemented my attachment to her. I cannot say what it did for her, but I was never the same again.

Many years later, someone in a therapy group said I married the first girl who ever let me kiss her. That was almost true. I was kissed on the cheek by a girl in second grade while waiting for the bus, and the teacher made me sit in the corner facing the wall until the bus came. I probably kissed two girls in high school. Once, while necking in the car with Jean in her driveway, she pressed into my mouth so hard my teeth cut into my lip. She said she liked being with me because she felt safe. It was all from the neck up. I went home feeling not so good. They called it blue balls. I had no interest in dating girls at the Air Force base as did many of the guys; girls were bused in from colleges for weekend dances. After that kiss with Rosalene, my fantasies all were centered upon her. Except, one of the married instructors asked me to keep his just-graduated sister-in-law busy while she was there on vacation because he knew she would be safe with me. We rode bikes all over during my off-duty time. She sent me a token shirt that I kept for years even though Rosalene never liked it. Anyway, she smoked and drank so I was not interested.

Mr. Hobart arranged for me to buy a used car that was repossessed by a local bank, even volunteering to cosign for me. I got a used 1951 Mercury Monterey—my first car—with fond hopes I could pay for it by the end of my service. I babysat for his four daughters sometimes, and that was a very welcome taste of home life off the base. They ranged in age from twelve down to four. The youngest one held out her hand and said, "My name is Connie, what is yours?" My duty fell into a mild routine teaching the evening shift, which gave me plenty of time to stroll over to the Biloxi beach and hang out during the day, always alone. During the fall of 1953, it became apparent that I would be assigned to field duty, most likely in Alaska on a remote mountaintop watching for an attack from Russia. That did not seem appealing to me so I took the opportunity of volunteering for flight duty since it meant another school and the possibility of staying in the states where I could go home every six months.

My letters to Rosalene became a way of life, although hers were mostly filled up with newspaper clippings and a short note about attending college classes at James Madison University in Harrisonburg, Virginia. She never liked to write letters and would ask me what to say when she wrote to her parents. Meantime, her parents had relocated to a church in Midland, Virginia, and her mother invited me to spend some time there during my summer 1953 leave. This seemed to close our relationship for me, and there was no doubt of some mutual acceptance by her as well—certainly also by her mother who must have seen something desirable in me.

Then came flight school and a new set of technical skills when I returned. I was quite proud of that, including marching a flight of troops to class each day as their barracks chief. Too bad that my family never got to see it. Thus, I returned for Christmas leave 1953 with a new set of flight wings and the uncertainty of where I would be assigned next. However, that turned out to be Ramey AFB on the northwest corner of Puerto Rico. The notion quickly arose that if we were married, Rosalene would be eligible for a dependent's allotment and possibly qualify for some time there with me during school vacations while she finished college. Rosalene sent me a white study Bible, which I read during quiet times in the loneliness of my room, and I accepted the concept that I was a sinner who needed the saving grace of Jesus Christ.

Her mother and father concurred in the plan and treated me like a son, provided that she finished college. When I went home again the end of January 1954 in preparation for my departure, we had a little ceremony where she accepted the modest engagement ring I had bought at the base PX. After I earned a little money several years later, I replaced it with one of more suitable size. I told her I did not know what I would do in the future, but whatever I did would all be for her. Next day, her mother baked my first birthday cake. On the same day, January 31, I was baptized by her father into the Church of the Brethren at the United Methodist church in Warrenton, Virginia, because they had no baptistry in the small country church—before a small group of witnesses—keeping my promise to myself. I put the car in storage in a garage near my home and departed for flight duty with Strategic Air Command in Puerto Rico. The letters now became more frequent. Mine were long diaries of my daily activities, but hers were short notes usually written during class supplemented with newspaper clippings I could not care less about.

Her mother made the wedding arrangements for the coming summer, and thus it was that we were married on Saturday, August 14, 1954, on my summer leave. Her father performed the ceremony in a church near Winchester, Virginia, that was packed with the members and onlookers wanting to check out the young airman who had snatched the preacher's daughter. I recall very clearly our first honeymoon night in a cabin along a gurgling stream at a motel near my hometown. It went perfectly for both of us. The base chaplain, Major Westlake, had told me a young man should not get married unless he could not help himself, and that described me. I just had to do it. He referred me to a book in the base library, and it provided the bulk of my sexual education.

We had a driving honeymoon through Pennsylvania that Rosalene arranged, and I was abruptly called back to base with a telegram when we arrived back to her family's house in Midland, Virginia. The abrupt departure sank me into the first plight of depression, but it was not to be the last. Then there came a year of angst and daily letters in which I poured out my love and grief to Rosalene, and she replied with short notes and newspaper clippings. Did I say that before? There was no telephone service to Puerto Rico, but we withstood the separation while she finished college, and I flew around the sky practicing my airborne skills on an RB-36 bomber crew. My job was to search for enemy ground radar stations that needed to be destroyed. At first, I was assigned to a training crew that included judo and small arms weapons training as well as jungle and water survival schools. In both of those, I had accidents that could have been potentially life-threatening. On jungle survival, I fell into a stream loaded down with a backpack, and I almost drowned when the wet suit leaked during ocean survival.

After upgrading to a combat ready crew, the missions were very long; more than twenty-four hours. We reported for roll call with the aircraft commander, Capt. Johanson and my leader, Capt. Lucketts, at the plane at 1:00 a.m. and conducted the preflight testing. Before takeoff at 4:00 a.m., we rode a shuttle bus that took us to the flight line grill where I always bought a grilled egg and cheese with milk. After takeoff, we dozed four hours head down on the desktop while flying to Miami, where the mission began about 8:00 a.m. I had four work stations, three in the aft compartment and one in the forward radio compartment behind and below the flight deck. Transit fore and aft was through a tunnel that required pulling yourself on a dolly, which was tricky while wearing the parachute and gas mask. Once, I got stuck on the way back, and they had to come and get me.

There were three overhead bunks that we shared for naps during the flight, but the noise and vibration was so bad it was impossible to get much sleep. It was also very cold up at 45,000 feet, even though we were dressed in arctic flight suits. There was a "honey bucket" on board, but the first one to use it had to empty it, so I never saw anyone use it, except for the tube for a urinal. Meals onboard were cooked in a convection oven in prepared trays. We usually landed back at base in early morning the next day, just before daylight. After the much-needed latrine, there was a mission debriefing then a shower, steam sauna, and alcohol rub before breakfast. By then, the base was awake so there was little chance for any sleep that day. I must have performed well because Capt. Lucketts recommended me for promotion to staff sergeant, which included a course in leadership and academy style training for six weeks. I would have graduated first in my class except somebody put dirt in my rifle barrel before inspection, so I came in second. I never did find out who did it or why.

Then I was promoted into the noncommissioned officer (NCO) ranks and was relocated to a private room in the NCO barracks with food service at the NCO club. My third-floor room looked out over the ocean where I sometimes saw ships on the horizon. I would look to the northwest and imagine Rosalene being where I would like to be with her. I returned once in 1995 to Ramey and found the airmen's club and my barracks, which was an office for faculty of University of Puerto Rico classes. The base was turned into a commercial airport and housing for US Coast Guard personnel.

When I was off duty, I devoted my time to reading at the base library and as a volunteer disc jockey at the base radio station, which some of my student fans from the base high school thought was my real assignment. I never really understood how they allowed me to do that, but I really enjoyed it. I also was active in the base chaplain program and occasionally worked out at the gym or attended movies at the base theater. I basically had only one friend, one named Hecht, who liked to take pictures as I did with the Argus C3 camera that my father-in-law bought for me. During the Christmas holidays 1954, Rosalene was able to come down for a visit. The chaplain arranged housing in base quarters vacated by school teachers who went home on leave. She packed a small artificial Christmas tree we set up on the table. After she graduated in summer 1955, she came back until I was released from active duty in September 1955. Did I say I wrote her daily long love letters, but her letters in reply were short and stuffed with newspaper clippings? Sorry, but I keep repeating myself.

We made friends with one career enlisted married couple named Sgt. Gerald and Diena Shepherd living on base who had two boys, Jimmy and Jerry. I babysat for them sometimes. It is hard to believe they are gone now, and the boys are senior citizens. After I was released, I had four more years of inactive reserve status. The records center at Denver burned up in a fire, so they never did issue me an honorable discharge, only a certificate of honorable service and orders on my Form DD-214. I suppose the Air Force experience defined my self-image for years to come. You did your job, obeyed the rules, and got promoted as your time in grade matured. I foolishly expected the civilian world to work the same way. I had no career plans, so I attempted to pursue the same line of work I did in the USAF, which involved some occupation in electronics. I might have stayed in the Air Force, but when I imagined Rosalene sleeping in her college dorm while we practiced bombing people, I just could not do it. I kind of wish I had kept my blue uniform, but all I saved were my dog tags, stripes, wings, and ribbons after I was released.

While I was trying to figure out what to do after my release, Rosalene's brother had enrolled in the Capitol Radio Engineering Institute in Washington DC. Although I had GI Bill education financial support for four years, its phrase, "An income producing education in a minimum of time," sold me. I enrolled there with some advanced standing credited for my training in the Air Force and some home study work I completed at the base. We found a furnished apartment on Newton Street within walking distance of the school located at Sixteenth Street and Park Road, and Rosalene took a job in retailing with Woodward & Lothrop, the Macy's department store of Washington at the time. She was offered a career appointment with the Department of Agriculture from her degree in home economics, but that had no appeal for her. Later, I learned she only majored in home economics because her mother told her to, and she always obeyed her mother. When I asked if her mother told her to marry me, she replied, "I'm not telling you." However, she did like sewing and preferred to make her own clothes.

I know she had boyfriends before me. One of them was going to seminary and did not believe a preacher's wife needed to go to college, so she dropped him. She never wanted to be a preacher's wife after she saw the glasshouse her parents had to live in. If she went on a date Saturday night, the whole church was talking about it on Sunday morning. She liked to lay back around the house in shorts and flip-flops and her hair in curlers, sometimes sans underwear, without fear some church members would drop in unannounced. Her mother and father always dressed in Sunday clothes every day, and she did not like that.

With my part-time job in meat cutting at a Safeway food store evenings and Saturdays and the GI Bill, we were able to save a little money while I went to school full time and she went to work. The only day of the week we had off together was Sunday, and so we made the most of it by either attending a church, driving out to Midland, Virginia, where her father was a pastor, to visit her parents, or taking in the sights of the nation's capital, museums, parks, the zoo, and such.

I graduated with an associate in science degree with honors in March 1957. The job placement officer located a job in DC with a consulting radio engineer, but it did not seem right for me, so I referred him to Rosalene's brother. He ended up taking it and developing it into a successful engineering business, including a radio station in Warrenton, Virginia. That was a critical decision for both of us. Like the late baseball star, Yogi Berra said, "Sometimes, you come to a fork in the road and you have to take it." I took a top-secret defense security job with RCA Service Company in Alexandria, Virginia, and we bought a newly constructed small ranch house at Edsall Park, about ten miles south of the Pentagon. I recall wondering why anyone would want to live that far from the city.

I had also received a job offer with a startup computer company in Pasadena, California, and I often wonder how my life might have turned out if we had moved there, or I had taken the job in DC. Rosalene was ready to move, but I did not want to leave her family. This decision was to be the first of several I made that I later realized must have been the will of God for my life, or it would be different. So, my doubts about free will started early. We traded the Mercury for a used cute red and white 1955 Chevrolet Bel Aire two-door car and bought a small Chihuahua dog we named Skipper—named for Rosalene because her father called her Skippy. Life settled into a blissful second honeymoon. I planted a hedge row around the house, which is there to this day.

We joined the newly constructed Church of the Brethren in Woodbridge, Virginia, and were so diligent that we were ordained as deacons by Pastor Harold Mason in 1958, nearly unheard of for being so young. He also presided at the official dedication of our house. However, during a construction project at the church, I suffered a bad back sprain that put me into a brace for six months—the first time I experienced severe pain. Once during a Saturday family visit, Rosalene's father said to me, "Well, Lew, you have your education, you have your job, and you have your home, so now you can start your family." I guess he was giving me permission.

It was apparent that Rosalene was not a career woman and was eager to leave the daily grind of her job. She would cry about the personal conflicts among the ladies she worked with. I told her she could quit, and we would make out on my income. I barely earned enough at $5,600 annually to pay all the bills, but she took my suggestion and quit immediately, never to work full time again. She also induced me to get her pregnant, and our daughter was born on August 9, 1959. I swear it was not my idea. Rosalene could not nurse because her nipples were blocked, so the doctor gave her some medicine to dry up her milk, and we bottle-fed the baby. She was precocious from the beginning. She skipped crawling and pulled herself up in the crib and walked around the edge. She threw her pacifier and diaper in the trash and zipped through potty training. She would not let us teach her how to tie her shoe laces because she said, "I can do it myself." The car had a major transmission failure, and I traded up to a new 1958 Mercury. It was certainly "snazzy," but it only got fourteen miles per gallon, and I had difficulty making the payments so in a few months, I traded backwards to a used 1953 Oldsmobile. This was to be the first of my financial lessons in life. Never borrow more than you can afford to pay back.

During my third annual performance review, my manager informed me that RCA would never give me any better status than a junior engineer rating because I lacked a BS degree. With that blockade and a nonworking wife and baby daughter, I began a new job search, which led to an offer with Raytheon Company in the Boston area. They offered the same salary I was making and full relocation expense, and it seemed like a much better opportunity. Rosalene said, "It's up to you, Lew. I will go anywhere you want to because you must make the living." Well, with that, I accepted the offer, sold the house, and packed up my small family and moved in the dead of winter, arriving in Waltham, Massachusetts, in early February 1960. Her mother was not happy with our move and cried the last time I visited them before we left. When I checked in with Raytheon personnel office, I got the next great shock of my life.

The job I was offered never existed, the man who made me the offer was gone, and they did not know what to do with me. Again, I felt the spear of depression as I had during the year of separation after our honeymoon. This was my first awareness that "do this, get that" sometimes does not work out. I had lost my home and my church and all that was dear to me chasing a dream that never existed. My self-loathing was acute and threatened my survival. Nevertheless, they honored the offer which I had in writing and arranged a job for me in application engineering for long range microwave communications, which was a better job than I had at RCA. They gave me a raise, and it seemed like the job change might be okay. However, our home life was a disaster in my opinion. Here is an aside: when we unpacked after the move, the pungent aroma of ammonia permeated everything because the numskulls had packed the full dirty-diaper hamper in with the clothing.

We tried to buy a new house in Saxonville, Massachusetts, that did not pan out well because they misrepresented the lot size, so we settled into a rented two-bedroom apartment in Framingham. Our daughter learned to walk and talk there, picking up the beginnings of a Boston accent. Rosalene never complained or criticized me for the move. On the contrary, she seemed to like the new adventure, including the winter snows in Massachusetts. I walked around the block on lunch hour, crying with self-loathing for my dismal situation. She realized how much I was suffering, and she made an appointment for me to see a psychiatrist who scolded me saying, "You are acting like a kid who had his favorite toy taken away. Now get to work and take care of your wife and child." However, my homesickness was acute, and each long holiday weekend, I packed up the wife and baby for a long drive back to Virginia. Her mother and father visited us once and seemed to be accepting my decision to relocate. I visited my own family once and gave my mother the only opportunity she had to hold her baby granddaughter at Easter time in 1960. My father wrote me a thank-you letter, which is the only one from him I have. He referenced Ephesians 5 as instructions on marriage life. I framed it for safekeeping.

My mother suffered a massive stroke in December 1960 and died in three days. The solo trip home was an excruciating mix of remorse and shock. When I returned to Boston, the airport parking lot was snowed in, and I had to work hard digging out my car. That helped to cement my resolve to return to Virginia. My brother and his wife and daughter moved in with my father, and life there was never normal again because they soon had my father moved out into boarding houses. Rosalene took my malaise in stride and usually arranged for sightseeing around the Boston area on weekends. We bought a new 1960 Rambler station wagon, and I enrolled in a sales management class at the University of Massachusetts at Harvard and tried to make the most of my job. I was given a new assignment and a raise with a much longer commute all the way to Norwood, Massachusetts, but I never missed a day for bad weather or snowstorms. I wrote a letter to the Boston Globe critical of the local politics for which I was reprimanded at work. We never found a church that made us feel welcome. It soon became apparent that life would be different in MA than anything I expected.

I began searching for a way to return to Virginia as that was the only solution that I could imagine living with. Eventually, I landed a technical sales job with a new startup company named DevTek located in Orlando, Florida, for the Washington area. It included relocation expenses and a company car. However, this too was another disappointment.

We moved back to Virginia in June 1961 and bought a small house in the town of Springfield, which again permitted us to attend our family church in Woodbridge. The pastor was helpful in alleviating my remorse and guilt for leaving, but I still had difficulty forgiving myself. Rosalene bought a piano and, eventually, an electronic organ and converted the downstairs rec room into a music center, which she used often, mostly playing her favorite hymns. Then Rosalene was pregnant for the second time, and I had to work out of the spare room in the house as my employer could/would not afford a formal office rental. I tried hard to make sales of custom-made printed circuit boards, but absolutely nothing happened, and in six months during November 1961, DevTek went bankrupt and closed its doors. Construction on the capital beltway behind the house was completed, which flooded our home with incessant noise from the traffic. I resolved to move soon, but we lived there for eleven years before that was possible.

Once again, my plan for "do this, get that" had not worked out. However, during my local area sales calls, I was acquainted with a new Washington DC branch of Sanders Associates, Inc., located from Nashua, New Hampshire, which was formed by a group of engineers from Raytheon. They employed me as the sales engineer for a new line of microwave lab products and thus saved me from a new pending disaster. Our son was born on December 21, 1961. He came home on Christmas day. Unlike his sister, who hit the road running, he was reluctant to enter the world and had difficulty learning to crawl. He suffered with indigestion and colic for several months that threatened his life until he was more fully developed, which gave us much concern and many sleepless nights. He would scream and turn blue until the colic attack subsided. We discovered he could digest goat milk, so I had to special order it for him at the drug store. Thankfully, he outgrew those challenges and became a healthy little boy. Rosalene became pregnant again almost immediately, but this time, she had a miscarriage. I was glad that I would not be responsible for a third child. I began to think about getting a vasectomy.

I worked for Sanders Associates, Inc. (1961–1965) first from the house, then from a small rented office in Springfield, Virginia, and then in an office they rented at 1751 Pennsylvania Avenue. From my window there, I could look down upon the backyard of the White House so I could see the presidential helicopters landing.

I also was able to view the parades along the avenue during holiday events. We enjoyed evening concerts by the various official military bands at the water borne barge moored off the Lincoln Memorial at Watergate and generally had a good time as regular residents in the Capital area. I found a college that accepted my credits and began a new curriculum part time in business administration at Southeastern University, which held night classes near the office. I thought I was positioned for a permanent career with Sanders as I made monthly trips to headquarters in Nashua, New Hampshire, and met with higher level officials in the company. But, once again, my destiny was to be disappointment with plans that did not work out, as I reached my "Peter Principle" level—getting promoted to your first level of incompetence.

In June of 1963, Rosalene's mother was stricken with a massive stroke and died in three days as my own mother had, but she was only age fifty-five. Rosalene often said she would not live as long as her mother did, and it proved to be true. This was a devastating shock to us and left her father in a dilemma that was the beginning of the end of his ministerial career. He was totally pampered by his wife and thus was emotionally destitute. A year later, he married Ruth, a widow from his church, and then he was obliged to resign from his pastorate. He never regained a full-time ministry and had to take a job in retail men's clothing while serving as a substitute Sunday preacher for his remaining work life. With her money, they bought a small house, and he began a model train hobby with a set her boss had given to Rosalene previously. Rosalene helped him set it up in the basement, where he often enjoyed playing railroad engineer. Both Rosalene and her father were railroad buffs from their years living in western Maryland. She ran a small N-gauge model setup in our own rec room.

She became discontent with our church family and the long trek to Woodbridge. She decided to relocate our membership to the First Baptist Church of Springfield in 1965 so the kids would have a more convenient church experience. We took active roles in the church, which included my appointment as a Sunday school teacher for the married couples' class. Rosalene worked in the day school for several years until she got another job teaching kindergarten in a private school where she worked for eight years. She liked teaching and was able to manage a classroom without any volunteer aides. Her forte was using hand puppets—many hand puppets—as teaching aids. She wanted to be home when school ended to be present for our own children. During one of my regular trips to Sanders headquarters in Nashua, they informed me the DC office was being taken over by someone with more senior credentials. My only option was relocation either to New Hampshire or to a plant on Long Island, New York. Since I did not like either option, I was once again left out and needed to find a new job.

This time, I landed a marketing engineer position in the summer of 1965 with a local area startup company named Scope, Inc. They were in the process of expanding to a new facility in Reston, Virginia. I began to chase government contracts and later was appointed as the manager of a new logistical support department, which required me to hire sixty-eight people and set up their administration. I had to rush downtown from work to attended classes, which often meant my family was sleeping when I got home. I graduated from Southeastern University in 1968 with the highest grades (summa cum laude) at the age of thirty-five, completing the college education I had deferred so long. They could not give me the academic key because I was an exchange student, but the president gave me one in person anyway because he said I deserved it. Since the university was chartered in Washington DC in 1879, the diploma read, "By virtue of authority granted by the Congress of the United States of America…" I bought myself a new 1968 Chevrolet Camaro, beige with gold interior, for my graduation gift. I often wish I still had that car because it became a classic collectable.

During those years of school and work, I had little time for family life, but Rosalene never complained about my absence and took care of the children in order to make it possible for me to complete my studies. I often did not get home until after they were all in bed, only to get up and do it over the next day. When I was ready to quit, she arranged a visit from a church deacon who told me if I continued, I would eventually outlive it. That motivated me to continue. But we did take vacations. One was a camping trip through the mountains of Kentucky and West Virginia. We were in mountains so deep there were no radio stations to be heard. Another was a drive to all the tourist attractions in Florida in our 1965 Dynamic 88 Oldsmobile in June 1969. That was the most powerful car I ever drove. But it was only one of twenty-five that I eventually owned. However, the kids fought so much I decided that would be the end of family vacations. Family troubles were just beginning.

Rosalene discovered a new mountain retreat area in the early 1960s called Shawnee Land, being developed west of Winchester where we bought some land, expecting that maybe we could one day build a cabin there for weekend retreats. We camped there many weekends hoping our dream might come true. She loved the outdoors and had us camping in the early spring until winter. We set up a large tent with cots and propane lantern, heater, and stove. I often did my homework under the trees on a picnic table while she entertained the kids. She especially liked to rent a gentle horse named Buckskin from the stable for strolling and to shoot at cans and bottles on the rifle range. They also had a tennis court and nine-hole golf course, but I had little time for that. The kids learned to get wet in the swimming pool at the lodge, often accompanied by Rosalene's Uncle Glen, who had built a house and retired early from the US Postal Service to live there. After her death, I sold the property to him. During the peak of those years, 1968–1970, I managed a department of sixty-eight people at Scope, Inc., most of whom I personally hired. It seemed like my business career finally was assured, but again, there was to be a new shocking development beyond my control. As the late assassinated Beatle, John Lennon said, "Life is what happens as you are making other plans."

When the war in Vietnam wound down, our government defense work declined, and they could not replace it with any commercial business, although they tried to acquire some other companies that did not work out. I had to lay off all the people whom I had hired, something I found very distasteful. That experience stifled my ambition to be an executive because I could not be ruthless enough. So, in June 1971, I once again found myself looking for another job.

Only this time, my personal resolve and confidence had been shaken with three surgeries that spring. One was a badly cut wrist from a home improvement accident, another was a complicated surgery for hemorrhoids. Instead of a routine procedure, I was hospitalized for twelve days. For the first time in my life, I experienced pain that absorbed my will to live. I also learned the meaning of humiliation and embarrassment. That experience was so traumatic that I experienced what it feels like to wish I were dead. I had a vasectomy also that had complications, but after the healing, both the quality and frequency of our sex life increased dramatically.

This was the first time I was ever hospitalized, and the experience left me with an awareness that very harmful things can happen to the human body over which we have no control. But I slowly recovered and then ran into the end of my job at Scope, Inc. My youth was gone, and I had begun what were to be the years of maturing. I began to realize a pattern of losses was presiding over my life that was very troubling, but these merely were preliminary to the main events yet to come.

PART II

Maturity and Beyond

I draw a line here between two phases of my life. On the one hand, my career finally found some traction, the family matured, and my roles in the church provided a grounding in scriptures. As a teacher of married couples, I was given some status as their mentor, which fed into my ego needs. It also acquainted me with scriptures beyond the traditional pulpit sermons. I also served on several committees, so we were involved with church activities several times a week. Rosalene did not mind my absences because I was "doing the Lord's work." On the other hand, (there always is another hand) it was a time of shock and awe. My change in employment required incipient skills that required me to muster up all the resilience I could find. It also was a time that brought challenges into my life that threatened my career and my faith. You might say I was like Job, allowed to lose all that I built to test my loyalty. But I was not Job so I could not say as he did, "The Lord gave and the Lord has taken away. Praise the name of the Lord" (Job 1:21). No way. It was more like this: "Though you build your nest high as the eagles, from there I will bring you down, declares the Lord" (Jer. 49:16, Obad. 1:4). This is not a God to be worshipped, but rather one to be feared. "When times are good be happy but when times are bad, consider this: God has made the one as well as the other" (Eccles. 7:14).

The Years at NECA

This time, I resolved to look for a job with more permanence outside the defense industry that might provide a way to use my recent business education, and the opportunity came in the form of a position with the National Electrical Contractors Association (NECA). After a six-month search and some better qualified competition than I, they surprisingly chose me as the new manager for marketing services. God works in mysterious ways. The choice was unusual as I had no track record of employment with associations, no connections with organized labor, and no knowledge about the business or its construction industry. But after several interviews including a lengthy evaluation by a psychologist, they actually granted me a large raise in pay. My starting salary was $18,000 beginning on July 17, 1971, reporting to Harold Winston, director of services. However, benefits always come with burdens. My years at NECA comprised the central time of my life so it takes a while to disclose all of it. Thanks for your indulgence.

NECA is a membership organization for the benefit of unionized electrical contractors organized from 1901 into 118 local area chapters all across the country. Headquarters operations are located in Bethesda, Maryland. Although the technology involved was electric power construction and not electronics, I found it very interesting, so I took some refresher courses at George Washington University to learn more about their line of work. I learned that without electrical contractors, buildings would be hot in summer, cold in winter, and dark all the time. Factories could not operate, and communications would be by messenger and smoke signals. Their work begins at the electric meter and continues to the desktop and shop floor. We tend to take electricity for granted, until it goes off, but we could not live without the wires and cables that bring it to our lives.

I also found some books in the library that helped to explain the construction business and the role of electrical contractors in the marketplace for electrical products. For the first time, I could use both my technical and business education with the potential for long-term employment. The primary downside was a long commute every day into DC by bus and traveling extensively around the country to attend various meetings representing the industry with other associations for electrical equipment manufacturing, wholesale distribution, and electric utilities. The association national convention provided a vacation for Rosalene, when she could go with me. Some might call such traveling a plus, but I cherished time with my family since I had spent so many years in school, and each day away from them renewed the feelings of despair that was ingrained from all the lost expectations I had in the past. And thus, I came at the age of thirty-eight to what they call another growth experience that tested my resilience.

During the first few years at NECA, I was thrust into a new environment of unionized labor facing the International Brotherhood of Electrical Workers (IBEW) that I had never experienced before. Also, the association was bound with traditions that ran back to its founding in 1901, so I found it more like an institution than an organization. Instead of rapid turnover, I found staffing loyalties and political boundaries that seemed to rule me out. It became obvious that I would have to earn my own position of trust and acceptance through flawless performance and impeccable behavior, which could take years. I was acutely aware of the possible impact of any mistakes I might make, both of commission or omission. It felt like walking on egg shells or through a mine field.

In addition, my boss had been promoted up from holding the position for seven years, and he had not fully released from the job, so he took more than the usual interest in supervising everything that I did. He emphasized several times that he had a graduate degree in econometrics, plus he was an amateur boxer while in the Air Force. One coworker who soon left described him as someone who had "the tact of a cleaver." That situation often left me feeling inadequate and wondering if I could ever live up to his approval. I felt depressed and afraid most of the time. Then, after about three years while I was on a trip to New York, he was abruptly fired. The shock was two-fold. One was surprise that one who seemed to be well accepted and highly qualified could be dropped so quickly for some political infraction, and the other was how could I avoid a similar fate without his support. But as it turned out, the tide of destiny was finally turning a little bit in my direction. I began to respect the NECA/IBEW relationship as a role model for labor relations that is not nearly as well-known as it should be.

The man who was assigned the job as my new boss was Mr. Richard L. Atwood. He had been the manager of the NECA chapter in Spokane, Washington, for twenty-three years and was brought to headquarters as special assistant to the executive director, Mr. Robert L. Hagen. Hagen was the son-in-law of the previous executive. I soon learned that such family nepotism was not unusual among construction trade unions, and that only made me more sensitive to my status as a rank outsider. Here is one example. During the first national staff meeting during the convention I attended, there was a discussion about pilfering small tools from job sites. Mr. Hagen asked anyone who never stole anything from his employer to stand up. Naturally, I stood up and immediately found myself all alone. He bellowed out, "So you are not only a thief, you are a damned liar also." I thought my job had ended before it began. Mr. Hagen (that is what everyone called him) was in the army during WWII, and he ran the place like a commanding officer. They called him a benevolent dictator.

Soon after I was hired, he handed me a two-volume three-ring binder report that had been prepared by some New York consulting firm hired about 1948 to reorganize the association after its near demise during the years of Depression and war. This report, which had been adopted as a long-range plan by the national executive committee at his recommendation, provided detailed recommendations for the organization that he was developing, including my own job description. I soon learned that he held controlling power of the association staff and that he respected the opinions and advice of my new boss. It appeared to me that Mr. Atwood could be the mentor that I needed to successfully survive in this new world. And it turned out to be so.

For example, I could scarcely do anything pleasing to Winston without making several revisions. After a staff member named Sandy Brownward unexpectedly died and I was asked to complete his assignment, i.e., writing a training manual for contractor financial management, I was both thrilled and scared. Sandy had been a field management consultant and taught me a lot about the industry practices during our frequent lunches together. He also taught me a lot about management education of business owners, which requires more than a teaspoon of entertainment to make the medicine go down. I knew only what I had learned in my recent college studies, and I had no contacts in the industry to validate my work. But when I completed writing the finance manual, Mr. Atwood boosted my self-confidence by saying, "This is excellent and just what is needed." I thought he should know.

After the untimely death of Sandy, they let me add on his workload to my own for five years, including collecting industry financial data and conducting executive management seminars until they were pressured to hire someone to replace him. However, I felt very insecure and uncertain about my future in the organized labor segment of construction. It was a time when a struggle was underway for power and control, and the IBEW was very uncooperative and vindictive. Also, in 1971, President Nixon supported the expansion of the vocational training centers in community colleges to provide a source of competing labor for nonunion contractors as a means of stifling the ever-growing demands of organized labor. There were news reports of some job site violence and destruction of property, but thankfully, they did not impact my job.

Meantime, there were other shocks at home. They moved the office from downtown to a location on Wisconsin Avenue in Bethesda, Maryland. I suffered through the commute on the Capital Beltway both ways and began searching for a house closer to Bethesda. After a year of fruitless effort and finally settling on a possible purchase, Rosalene made her opposition clear by crying and lamenting, "Please don't move me over here with all these old Marylanders." She was a

MY RESURRECTION FROM HELL

Virginia lady, through and through. So, we ended up moving to our last home in Springfield in February 1973, and I continued through the daily twenty-one-mile commute on the Capital Beltway, fuming all the way. The move was difficult for the children as they had to change schools in the middle of the year. My son lost his best friend and never quite recovered from the shock. My daughter said later that kids were selling drugs in her middle school. Moving without preparing the kids was possibly my greatest regret as a parent. It just never occurred to me to involve the kids in the plans to move and neither did Rosalene mention it.

My father died in November 1972, and my brother and his second wife took over all the property. During one of my last visits with him, he said, "Well, Lewis, we could talk about the past, but it would not change anything, and I think I did the best that I could under the circumstances." I hope that I did also. They signed over his property and moved him into a public nursing facility after placing him in a couple of boarding houses for several years. There was nothing more I could do except visit him as often as possible during his last few months, dragging my wife and kids along for the ride. He never complained, but I could see that he was quite despondent near the end. He died with the Bible being his only possession, which I have as a keepsake. The only thing I got from the estate was a small table I did my school homework on while I listened to the radio. I would have liked the antique RCA Victrola phonograph and set of records though, but my brother discarded everything without consulting me.

Rosalene was diagnosed with breast cancer in the fall of 1975 and had a radical Halsted mastectomy on November 10, just after returning from the national NECA convention in New York. I say this matter of factly, but it was the biggest shock of our lives. As they took her to surgery, the doctor said if it was benign, she would return in less than an hour, but if not, it would take several hours. As I watched the clock go past two hours, I knew the worst had happened. The first thing Rosalene said upon waking was, "Did they take it all?" Rosalene attended a support group for cancer survivors and immediately became a volunteer. The next month, she was invited to appear on a local TV daytime show for her work in *Reach to Recovery*.

On the drive home from the rehearsal, I had an accident and hit a light pole along the Rock Creek Parkway next to the Watergate area of DC. The 1974 Ford Maverick was totaled, and Rosalene broke her right wrist. I had some cracked ribs and bruised kidneys, which were treated at George Washington University Hospital. With the insurance money, I bought a used 1970 Chevrolet Nova. I always owned two cars so Rosalene would have transportation while I worked. She always had the newer one. While I was away on a trip, my son converted the Nova suspension to a "dragster," and she thought it was neat. I made him return it to normal.

We got through the 1975–76 winter and welcomed spring trying to get life back to normal as though nothing had happened. Just as we had thought that life, work, school, and church had settled down, this blow was both physical and emotional to all of us, the children included. Her illness made it impossible for me to relocate again because my insurance advisor said that she would be excluded from further medical coverage under the preexisting exemptions rule. In addition, both kids needed extensive orthodontist treatments for their teeth and that added another financial burden. I consulted with the president of my alma mater, and he gave me some fatherly advice saying, "Well, it seems like you have to stay there so why not just work on making it better." And that is what I did.

While carpooling with him during the infamous oil embargo that created a gasoline shortage around 1973–74, I gained the support of the industry trade magazine publisher, and I began writing a monthly byline series of marketing articles for the electrical contractors. I also traveled with him annually to present the latest industry developments to manufacturing companies advertising managers, which helped to sell the magazine advertising services. Slowly, my career seemed to be settling in for the long haul.

Although she had to wear a bra prosthesis, Rosalene tried to keep life as normal as possible for me and the kids. But in private, things were different. She was uncomfortable lying in bed, so I added a single bed, and we never slept together again. Rosalene wore a size 36-D bra so she really hated the prosthesis and threw it across the bedroom one time. Sex changed as we had to accommodate to her least uncomfortable positions, but it continued. She had arranged for us to usher at the new Wolf Trap Farm Park for performing arts in the summers, and we enjoyed many professional performances for four seasons. But we had to abandon that after her surgery. We remained active in the church, and she studied theater production and set up a drama program. She sold the budget, arranged for stage construction, researched plays, and organized and directed various productions for the seasons. Rosalene supported foreign mission work, and, before the end, she was planning to spend a summer volunteering in Alaska when another crisis occurred. Rosalene suffered an acute attack of painful bursitis in her right shoulder that was so disabling she could not dress herself for several months. The only effective treatment was radiation that I wondered might have contributed to her demise as a side effect.

After regular checkups every three months for five years, just as when we thought the cancer threat was over, the surgeon detected an ominous change in her blood count and referred us to a partnership of three oncology specialists. They referred us to the National Institutes of Health (NIH) where they diagnosed a rare type of bone marrow disorder, likely inherited from her French Huguenot ancestors. They sent us back to the oncologists for the only treatment available—periodic blood transfusions that extended her life another five years. We went on as best as we could. She liked to attend the conventions with the sights and sounds and scenic tours attached. She would take an empty suitcase to hold the souvenirs that she brought home.

Although I followed Rosalene into whatever faith she chose, I also extended my Bible studies beyond the lectionary provided in the class leaders' guides. She bought a *Thompson Chain Reference Bible* for me that greatly facilitated my lesson preparation. It began to open my understanding toward the eventual discovery of the principle of "proof texting" the Bible. I discovered that much of Christian dogma is promoted by cherry-picking one-sided scriptures to prove the point. I won't mention any names, but I call them "prosperity preachers." They like to quote specific scriptures meant for that time and place and convert them into broad generalities as though they are meant for everyone. It works and helps to fill their megachurches each Sunday and supports their television programming.

As I studied more, it became obvious to me that the Bible contains two sides to many basic issues that you will not get in church. I will cite one blatant example here. The basic Christian dogma is presented in this scripture in third person: "God so loved the world that he gave his only begotten son so that whoever believes in him will not perish but have everlasting life" (John 3:16). This reads as though people have free will to believe or not. However, recorded in the same book is this scripture quoting Jesus in first person. "No one can come to me unless the Father enables/calls them" (John 6:44, 65). He also said to his disciples, "You did not choose me, I chose you" (John 15:16, 19). The disciples of Jesus are referred to as "the chosen/called" throughout the New Testament. Where is the free will? But the Bible says God is not the author/creator of confusion/disorder, so who is? (1 Cor. 14:33, KJV). Elsewhere, it says with God, nothing is impossible, which must include breast cancer (Luke 1:37). God has a lot of explaining to do. I discussed the many flaws in the Bible in my book titled, *The Bible You Don't Get in Church*.

After Rosalene died, I needed to find an answer to the ubiquitous question, "Why?" Gradually, I found the solution or maybe it found me. As I learned more, my vision of God changed until I saw it as the prime force in the universe, the God above all gods, the generator, operator, destroyer of everything from atoms to galaxies. The complete discussion of my discovery follows in part four.

Meantime, my daughter graduated from high school in 1977 and began attending George Mason University located about six miles from our house. I could not afford to send her away to school and thought it best that she should spend as much time as possible with her sick mother. The kids never were close, and her incessant bullying behavior made my son feel glad that she was not around much. I bought her a small 1975 Honda Civic car to commute, and she got part-time jobs, one clerking in a dry-cleaning shop and another as teller in a bank. Her mother involved her in the church drama program, which was to initiate a family crisis later on.

MY RESURRECTION FROM HELL

My son never was a good student, especially after we bought another house in 1973 to get away from the beltway traffic noise, which required them both to relocate to different middle schools during the winter term. The move required him to adapt to new friends and teachers and to leave his best friend behind in the middle of sixth grade, something he was unable to do as well as his sister did. We did not understand their need to grieve and so failed them both in their sorrow and mourning for lost friends. He preferred working with things to school book learning because he is not a "page turner." He took up making radio-controlled model airplanes after I started him with one at the suggestion of Rosalene. She wanted me to arrange some father-son bonding events, so I became the assistant coach for his soccer team. We would get up early on Saturday mornings to mark off the field before his games. Later, he obtained a paper route and maintained a perfect delivery record, and then he worked at a gasoline station after school. I bought him an American Gremlin car for college, which he promptly wrecked; so I gave him the title and told him to proceed as he wished. He enrolled in community college, but his heart never was in it. I think their mother's illness grossly impacted both kids more than we knew. The problem with education, as I see it, is students take the courses they like and end up working for whomever will give them a job.

My daughter made it through George Mason University, graduating in 1981 with a BS degree in business administration. She had a quick mind, but she relied upon memory instead of reason and so had difficulty with analytical courses. She tried an acting class but quit, claiming that she already knew all that. Plus, she liked to party because it made her feel popular. Her first real boyfriend was a drug dealer in high school, and she thought it was "neat" that he chose her. That was the beginning of her attraction to alcoholics whom she said were "very exciting." She loafed about for a while with different boyfriends until I encouraged her to move on. She got a job with ABC News and looked into moving to NYC but decided it was too cold. I wanted the kids to stay close to their mom so long as possible. But she moved out saying, "Why should I stay here and live by your rules, when I can move out and live by my own rules." The only rules were to be in bed by midnight on weekdays and to help pay the utility bills. It was sad for us to see both kids leaving the lifestyle in which they had been raised. The proverb, "Raise up a child in the way he should go and when he is older, he will not depart from it," is not true in all families (Prov. 22:6). Then abruptly in the fall of 1984, she changed her name and announced she was moving to Los Angeles (LA) to be an actress. Her move troubled Rosalene as she lived from one transfusion to another, and I tried to pretend it was okay.

After fifteen years in Los Angeles "having a blast," my daughter relocated to Nashville, Tennessee, claiming she was a going to get a record deal as country music artist. I visited her whenever I could, and took her on a few national conventions, but she rarely came home to visit. In one spell, we had no contact for four years, and in another, I did not see her for nine years. Relations with her brother were totally ruptured, and I fear my family will never be together again. Some things that are broken just cannot be fixed. I helped her buy a house in 2001. Her plans for a record deal failed, and in 2003, she was diagnosed with bipolar personality disorder. She managed to qualify for Social Security disability in 2003. By hosting three transient borders, she was able to remain in the house. She certainly is persistent and tenacious to get her needs met, and I applaud her ability to manage her life in the "new normal." After seeing what happened to me, neither kid ever wanted to marry or to have children.

Throughout the 1980s, I pursued my career at NECA with stoic discipline, I suppose from my air force training. Each year, I had to create a new program and sell it to management to gain budget approval. My job involved market research, sales training, national advertising, convention exhibits, and electrical industry relations, plus publishing a quarterly technical journal. I only had one assistant, so we had to hire independent freelance suppliers. I had to maintain relations with a national marketing committee of twelve electrical contractors from all over the country and obtain their support for my proposals. My job included hosting their wives for our meetings at expensive resorts around the country. It took me several years to get used to that part of my job. I organized a new national referral service to connect contractors with customers we called the NECA Connection that is still being implemented. As I had some success, my self-confidence improved.

My most important contribution was surveying new technical developments and steering the NECA members their way ahead of the competition. The development of fiber-optic communications cable began to create new business opportunities for the industry, and I was positioned to help make it happen. However, this required a multitasking team effort that was not traditional for the association. It required national awareness and acceptance by electrical contractors, changes in the union labor agreements, reclassifying of electrical contracting by the US Bureau of Census, as well as changes and new training products for the national apprenticeship program.

The breakup of AT&T and removal of its monopoly made it possible for new competitors to enter the communications industry, and that required educating NECA members about the potential in national marketing. My boss recognized the multibillion-dollar opportunity and supported my efforts to reach out in ways that expanded my job description as well as my perceived role. He also helped qualify me for annual raises. I was able, with his help, to gain the acceptance and support of the national apprenticeship training director in Upper Marlboro, Maryland, as well as to communicate through him and the magazine the new opportunities to the industry.

We had to get the US Bureau of Census to reclassify inside telephone wiring as electrical contracting to change the government policies and standards for that type of work. It also required gaining the awareness and acceptance of the newly organized Building Industry Consulting Service International (BICSI) composed of freelance telephone engineers. During my first presentation at their national convention in Florida suggesting they should partner with NECA, I was booed. But they soon adjusted and eventually helped to organize and populate a new BICSI certified training lab at the many NECA/IBEW training centers around the country. My work as a staff member was conducted behind the scene, so only the contractors on the national marketing committee and my boss knew what I was doing for the industry.

About that time, building digital controls systems also were introduced, and I used my role as editor and publisher of a technical journal called the Electrical Design Library to help promote the interest of NECA contractors. The additional advertising revenue potential from new suppliers was recognized, and additional sections were added to the trade magazine and to the convention trade show to accommodate them. In the middle of this effort, my boss was struck with colon cancer, and, although he continued working after surgery, his presence in my work was diminished so I was positioned with more freedom and less oversight. I like to think the work I did in those years helped to create some new jobs and added considerable additional revenue to the industry.

Then things changed again. We moved into a new building near the old one at the metro center in Bethesda, Maryland, where they gave me a small but adequate corner office. I made a minor negative comment about it to someone and a month later at the convention in New York City, the national president who was a contractor in Minnesota accosted me with, "Lew, I hear you are the only one who does not like the new building." This was another warning that the informal channels could destroy me if I wasn't more careful about any complaints. In 1985, Mr. Hagen announced his pending retirement and began a national search for his replacement. After a lengthy process, Mr. George M. Jackson was selected from his position as manager of the NECA chapter in Milwaukee, Wisconsin. After a year of understudy, he was appointed the new executive director in 1986, and with him, he brought a younger generation of ideas and policies. He was only thirty-six years old at the time, and I was age fifty-three.

Meantime, my boss announced his retirement and told me privately that he had recommended me for promotion to his job. However, Jackson selected a friend of his about his own age named Wilber Daniels. With his large black mustache, he always reminded me of Groucho Marx. He also reorganized the staff and assigned the magazine and the national convention staff to report to Mr. Daniels as chief operating officer. The magazine publisher retired, and so I was again placed at the bottom of a high totem pole that challenged my ability, working for managers twenty years younger than I. My mentor was gone, and I was on my own.

I taught the married couples' Sunday school class, and we sometimes attended special guest speakers and local theater and concerts. Rosalene liked pipe organs, having taken lessons with the piano at a funeral home during high school, and sometimes, we went to organ concerts in the area. Whenever possible, she would record them on her tape recorder and play them back later. Her tape player was a source of comfort during her last week in the hospital. I saved it among the box of her keepsake things along with a grubby pair of shoes she liked. Toward the ending, she said, "I am sorry this is taking so long," and all I could say was, "I am sorry it is happening at all." Rosalene had thirty pairs of shoes, fifteen purses, and five wigs in addition to three sewing machines and dozens of clothing patterns. It tore me apart to give them up. I invited her church friends to take what they wanted. Removing the personal contents of her closet and dresser was almost more than I could bear. I have known some widows who kept the house intact like a museum after their husbands died. Just writing about it makes me feel dizzy. Gradually, I was able to replace the bedroom and living room furniture, so I could have a different ambience of my own in which to live.

Rosalene tried to maintain a normal life even though there was an elephant in the house we tried to ignore. She bought a first-generation Atari computer to play with during her last year. She also enrolled us in a BASIC language programming class during June the year before she died, and she learned to produce weekly newsletters for some local churches. Afterward, I discovered she had written a short farewell note to me inside her notebook during classes that she never disclosed. Among other things, she wrote, "Enjoy the Laser, it is a nifty car." She had picked it out because she wanted a sports car instead of a "mom's car." If I had discarded the notebook without browsing through it, her note would have been lost.

The last time she ever went out was the weekend of July 4 as we attempted a drive to Black Water Falls in West Virginia, one her favorite locales for church camps during her high school years. We had to cancel the trip halfway there and return home because she was too weak. From then on, Rosalene just lounged on the sofa with her music tapes and watching television. She was ambulatory until she entered the hospital, which made her death an unexpected shock. She wanted to read the newspaper the last day on Sunday that she was conscious saying, "I think I should keep up with what is going on." She could not hold the paper, so I held it up for her to see the headlines. Rosalene was my window on the world, and after her loss, I had to become more open for myself to the wide varieties of life forms on earth and the many cosmic wonders in the creation of God.

That afternoon, she became unresponsive and never spoke again. I had attended church alone that morning and walked forward to ask the pastor to pray for me because "Rosalene is dying." Then he went on with the service as planned. Not a single person offered me any support or condolences. I did not learn until much later that Apostle Paul had instructed the churches to "carry each other's burdens" (Gal. 6:2). If I found a church group who practiced that, I might rejoin. In my experience, when you laugh, the world laughs with you, but when you cry, you cry alone.

Rosalene entered the hospital on August 10, 1985, at 3:00 p.m. At her checkup that morning, the doctor said, "Up until now you have not been in a life-threatening situation, but now you are. I can make three suggestions. You might take a short vacation and enter the hospital when you return. Or you might return home and try another round of chemo treatment. Or you could enter the hospital today so we can begin a more rigorous treatment." She looked at me and asked, "What must I do?" I said we will do whatever you want, and she asked the doctor when she should check in. On the final drive to the hospital in her "nifty" new silver Chrysler Laser sports car, I cried and lamented, "How am I ever going to continue working until I can retire without you?" And she replied, "Oh, by then you will have forgotten all about these times." As you can see, she was very wrong about that. Not only have I not forgotten, but also the hole in my heart has never healed. When somebody enters your heart like that, they never leave. The body of Rosalene may be gone, but the love remains. Each summer, I go through the memories of that time up until her death on Labor Day weekend. The heart never forgets.

Perhaps the feeling of being connected with a deceased loved one is evidence for a hypothesis that British biologist, Rupert Sheldrake, and others are calling "morphic energy." Morphic fields are created by morphic energy, and morphic energy is present at every point in the universe. Morphic energy is part of the so-called dark energy that is assumed in cosmology but still is undetectable. If energy can neither be created nor destroyed, the energy called life may be immortal and ever present after the body is reduced to basic elements of the earth. When morphic energy fields unite in resonance, a new entity is formed as in the combination of atoms into a new molecule in chemistry. Evidence is being discovered in physics, psychology, and medicine pointing to this possibility. We accept the theory of electromagnetic radiation to explain communications through space by invisible fields, which makes possible all those handheld cell phones and GPS navigation. So why not assume the existence of resonant energy fields of life that connect soul mates throughout space/time?

Perhaps Jesus tried to explain this by saying, "The spirit gives life, the flesh counts for nothing" (John 6:63). And he affirmed that in a true marriage an irrevocable merger occurs combining two souls into one as in conception where the egg and sperm unite. "What God has joined together let no one separate" (Matt. 19:5). Perhaps birth and death merely are transitions of energy/spirit from one form into another and back again. (www.sheldrake.org, *A New Science of Life*, 1995)

Rosalene died from a critical pseudomonas bacterial infection that caused fatal gangrene after her immune system failed. Her body broke out in large blisters from the inside out that looked like third-degree burns on her left side and arm. They considered possible surgical debridement—that is, scraping away the dead flesh—but it would only increase her suffering, so it was rejected. She was being treated with an experimental form of stem cell regeneration for aplastic anemia that rarely worked. They don't use it anymore. Her suffering was so great they put her into a coma the last three days to avoid the pain. We had decided she would not be put on life support. I will never lose the memory of her condition in the last days, seeing her body that I loved so much being eaten up like a rotting banana. The doctors gave us the impression that she might return home so on our anniversary date of August 14, with her brother and his wife visiting, she told me to save the cake they brought in the freezer so we could celebrate when she got home. I could never touch that cake, and eventually, I just discarded it. We got quite a few anniversary cards that Rosalene had me tape up on the wall surrounding a large mirror. She was so hopeful a nurse asked me, "Does your wife know how sick she really is?" One never forgets such things.

I visited the doctor afterward to complain that they had taken our good-bye time from us by not telling me the end was so near. They were absent on the Labor Day holiday, and I had to rely upon the nurses for information, which they were forbidden to disclose. He said, "Mr. Tagliaferre, all our patients die, but we cannot tell the exact time." That was no comfort to me at all. At one point, they sent a group of young interns to her room to "watch someone die."

When I told her that I would like to crawl into the bed and change places with her, she replied, "Oh no, you don't either." And once she commented, "I always loved you in my own way." Forgive me for repeating this, but I cannot forget it. I think she knew the time was short. When a nurse brought her child to visit her one night, Rosalene held the child on her lap and commented, "I would have made a good grandmother." She looked around the room and said, "Life comes down to a hospital room." The doctor suggested that I call our daughter who came in from Los Angeles for the weekend. As I drove to the airport early on Saturday morning before sunrise, the car was bathed in a golden light for a minute or so. I swear it was not the sunrise. When the attending nurse said at 7:15 p.m. on Tuesday evening, "It will not be long," my daughter bolted from the room. I found her on the phone at the nurses' station making an appointment for lunch the next day.

So, it was the nurse, her brother and his wife, and I who watched Rosalene die. The corpuscles in her skin began to rupture (called mottling), and her hands became cold and blue. She looked up at the clock on the wall as the last breath left her body. I wondered if she was checking the time of her death. It was about 7:21 p.m. on Tuesday evening, the day after Labor Day, September 3, 1985. I closed her eyes with my left hand and told her it was okay to go as the kids and I would be okay. What a fool I was. The nurse commented, "Wasn't that beautiful?" We stayed with her body until nearly midnight when they told us we had to leave so she could be removed to the hospital morgue before it closed. On the way out of the room, I tweaked her cold blue toe and said, "Good-bye, Rosalene." She always liked to sleep with one foot outside the covers. I never saw her again.

Rosalene had told me, "You are not as strong as you think you are." She also said, "I always loved you in my own way." And to one of her church friends, she had said, "I am afraid that Lew will become a basket case." She was right about that. We had a reunion meeting for church friends at the funeral home on Friday evening, and the room was full. My daughter returned to Los Angeles the day after the funeral. We had decided on cremation because we did not want the kids to envision our bodies rotting in a hole someplace.

After her cremation, her brother and I drove the next Monday to Westernport, Maryland, and deposited the ashes into the Potomac River near to where we had met for our first kiss. Later, I realized she never really liked that place. I have designated my ashes to be deposited near the same spot so they will be mingled with hers in the river. The following month, they arranged a memorial gathering for her at the church and while her friends expressed their memories, I felt sick to my stomach. As my son said, they were her friends and not mine. I drove her Laser for a year or so and then traded it for a 1986 Honda Accord. Buying cars has always kept me poor, but I just could not continue sitting in her seat in her favorite car. It was silver with a red interior, her favorite color.

Rosalene liked to sew and made most of her own clothes, which required a room full of what she called "my things." But she never pampered me and when my socks needed repairs, she would just hand me a needle and thread. Toward the end, she became a hoarder and would hardly dispose of anything with meaning for her. She left a lot of her things for me to painfully remove, which angered my son. He complained, "You are getting rid of Mom." She often complained that we needed a bigger house with more closets, and, if she were healthy, we might have moved up to a new contemporary neighborhood that she liked. In addition to the new younger NECA management, I had to contend with her gigantic loss, both for myself and for the children.

My son dropped out of college after taking six years in community college to do two, while he still lived at home. He was self-supporting by assembling printed circuit boards almost perfectly for some computer maker on a piece rate basis, cluttering up the lower level of my house. He was handsome as a male model and never wanted for female company. This arrangement went from bad to worse, and I encouraged him to move out to learn how to become independent. He bought a one-bedroom condo in Reston, Virginia, and went on with his career in technology until his last job with Sprint ended. Then he developed a successful business for himself in home remodeling after 2003. I am proud of his accomplishments, but I worry about his long-term outlook and old age security.

The next decade unfolded on two fronts. One was my career and the other was my personal life. While Rosalene was in the hospital, I obtained certification for the personality model called Myers-Briggs Type Indicator (MBTI), because she encouraged me saying, "We are still a team." The Holmes-Rahe scale of distress places death of a spouse at the top. The doctor had said, "It does not get any worse than this." I was very disoriented, feeling like had been dropped into a foreign country where I did not speak the language. My grieving distress was so severe after she died that I entered therapy to survive and there followed sessions with several different social workers, psychologists, and a psychiatrist for ten years. I tried various forms of therapy including cognitive behavior therapy, dialectical behavior therapy, schema therapy, and acceptance commitment therapy. None of them really helped me very much. The facts were that my wife was dead, my family was broken, the lifestyle I valued so highly was gone, and God was nowhere to be found. What I needed was reality therapy. I began reading all I could find on living a healthy life as a single widower.

As in Buddhism, the only solution to my crisis was acceptance of my new lifestyle, which I fought for to survive. My psychiatrist said, "I have never seen anyone work so hard on this as you." I had to or I would die.

There was no joy in going home at night, so I stayed in the office reading and writing until bedtime. I read all I could on grief and mourning to learn what was happening to me. And, with a coauthor who was a psychologist and seminary professor, I published *Recovery from Loss*, a book that uses the Myers-Briggs Type Indicator (MBTI) personality theory to help counselors coach mourners through grief. In it, we described five tasks of recovery: Acknowledging the loss, feeling the feelings, finding substitutes, detaching from the past, and reconstructing a new life. I realized very soon I was a naïve youth when it came to singles living so I began a reading campaign that resulted in writing a summary of all I learned about healthy singles living in a book titled, *Kisses aren't Contracts*, that I self-published. Later, that book was to play a crucial role in my life during recovery from my losses.

I was traveling some of the time conducting marketing training seminars and attending industry-related meetings. I was able to visit most of the states and many cities worth seeing, which gave me a wide awareness of this great country. This was good in that it got me out of the office and often presented new scenery and different people, so I was not confined with memories that pierced my heart all the time. However, all the socializing added additional stress to my introverted personality. They say the Chinese symbol of change includes both threat and opportunity. I was certainly living in that domain of yin and yang. My reputation was established nationwide, and my professional status was confirmed. It needed to be because the office was equipped with a new computer system for the first time for bookkeeping, project management, and communications in 1986. This development required that I spend extra hours after 5:00 p.m. to learn and master all the new technology. A few staff members were lost in the attempt. I tried to assure my new boss that I was working hard after hours to keep up, and he reassured me by saying, "We know you are committed to the technology." I must have been running on empty because I scarcely knew who I was anymore. I lost a lot of weight, and people wondered about my survival. The old person had died with Rosalene, but the new person had not yet been born. I was a ghost walking.

Then about 1989, a new opportunity was presented, which also proved to build me up only to let me down again.

Mr. Hagen had wanted for some time to organize a nonprofit foundation to fund new research and education for the industry, but he could never get it done. Mr. Jackson took up the goal and asked if I could attempt to organize it, and, naturally, I did not decline. This assignment could be the capstone of my career. This task required that I do extensive research on other association foundations to learn what worked and what did not. We also hired a fund-raising consultant and a lawyer for the legal matters—writing up the bylaws, getting IRS tax-exempt certification, and such. Overall, it took more than a year and George announced me as acting director. They published my appointment in the monthly magazine, so I thought my future was made. However, he soon discovered my fatal flaws were no experience in fund raising, and I had little enthusiasm for asking our business owners for $100,000 donations. I also had trouble remembering names and faces of people I rarely ever saw.

So, after providing me with a leased 1989 Buick and a reserved parking space, he reconsidered and brought in Mr. Alex Russell whom I had interviewed earlier during the research phase to run the foundation. He had fund-raising experience with the plumbing foundation. He was comfortable in the challenge involved in our new startup, plus he had an MBA degree. George let me buy the car for wholesale, but he took back the parking space for Alex. To my great relief, he let me keep the marketing job, which of course took a terrible load off my shoulders since I had eight years to go until my possible retirement. Actually, I was relieved because I had to admit I had again met my "Peter Principle" level of incompetence. My longtime secretary was ready to move up with me, but she took another job for more pay, which did not work out and later left the association. I often wonder what ever happened to her because I went through three pregnancies with that woman, and we were together all day sharing our troubles for twelve years.

I spent the remainder of my career at NECA doing the best I could with the marketing job. My traveling increased as I created and conducted a sales and marketing seminar through several revisions that were sponsored locally by the chapters. This increased my stage presence around the country and across Canada, but it also added stress because I never knew what contractor might not like my stuff and call headquarters to complain. Those were wet armpits days, for sure. However, that never happened, and I usually got excellent ratings. Along the way, there emerged another change. In 1978, Congress had enacted the existence of Labor-Management Cooperation Committees (LMCC). These were appended to existing labor law and authorized unions and employers to set up industry improvement funds jointly, something prohibited until then. The early adopters among NECA chapters began to organize such committees because they provided a new source of income. I could see them taking over much of my job in promoting the industry. It took a few years for the headquarters labor department managers to get the message, but they did and began funding similar projects as mine, especially industry advertising promotion.

More losses came quickly. The new foundation budget took over my roles in research and management education, so there was little remaining in my job to do. During the last year, I had surgery for a double hernia, which also seemed to be a sign that it was time to move on. Consequently, I planned to retire on my pending sixty-fifth birthday since staying longer would add little annually to my pension for each year more that I worked. And so that is what I did. On January 31, 1998, I left NECA in good hands as I enrolled for Social Security and the NECA-defined benefit pension plan. They gave me a lunch and the usual plaque certifying my "twenty-seven years of dedicated service." When I had interviewed for the job in 1971, Mr. Hagen tried to sell me on the value of the NECA pension, which he had worked very hard to secure for staff employees. I flippantly told him I did not ever plan on retiring, but he said, "Maybe you will think differently about it when you are age sixty-five." He was right. The defined benefit pension has been much appreciated as I am aware that most workers in America no longer have this benefit.

Soon after I retired, my son arranged for me to buy a small used motorcycle to get out of the house. That began a hobby of trading them often just for the novelty of riding different bikes—after I took the riders safety training course. During my last trip to Sedona, Arizona, to visit a retired high school classmate living in Las Vegas in December 2001, I fell and broke my left wrist along a roadside stop on Mt. Mingus to take some pictures. I have not been on an airplane since then. After that healed, I rode some large scooters with automatic transmissions that did not require grasping the clutch for shifting. When I quit riding, I had owned about twenty-six different motorcycles, none of them a Harley Davidson. I probably also owned as many cars, up to four at a time for each member of the family. I rode bikes all over the county, possibly as much as fifty thousand miles. I often packed a picnic lunch to eat at one of the many pleasant parks. I was always alone, of course, so I could practice being in the here and now and stimulating my senses in contrast to my usual mode of being inside my head all the time. This hobby worked out a lot better than my attempts at golf, which proved quickly that I am no more athletic now than I was in high school. For me, golf was a long walk in a park ruined by extensive frustration. My poor depth perception just made it impossible.

During my career, I traveled across Canada and all over the USA to all the states except Alaska, Oklahoma, and North Dakota, but I had little to no connection with my own residential area. However, and this is the good part, soon after I retired, I was given the opportunity to consult part time with the Washington DC, NECA chapter by its manager, Paul Andrews. This chapter was one of the early adopters of LMCC development, and he had just recently lost or ended the relationship with its communications provider. I contacted one of my freelance suppliers, Denise Wilson, and we organized to help the chapter spend its additional money effectively. I set up a home-based proprietorship named C-E-C Group and opened a business bank account. There followed twelve years of engagement providing much the same kind of research and sales promotion I had done, only now on the local level in the metro DC area, for one of the best managed and most successful chapters in the country. As such, I got to know the chapter operations more intimately than was possible from my headquarters position.

This engagement provided some much-appreciated extra income that I used to buy and trade those motorcycles, and it also kept me active with the industry, which was unusual among retirees. I always will be thankful to Paul for supporting me during that time, although I think it was a mutually satisfying arrangement. Possibly my most important contribution was getting the DC area contractors involved with the program for green building and certified for the Leadership in Energy Efficient Design (LEED) construction program.

During my post retirement years, I also was contracted to write a monthly series on energy policy matters for the e-book version of *Buildings* magazine, which assignment also kept me busy and involved for five years. Thus, all told, I was employed by the energy-related industry for nearly forty years.

During Rosalene's last week on earth, I was enrolled in a certification class on the Myers-Briggs Type Indicator. I think this personality model created by the late Swiss psychiatrist Carl G. Jung (1875–1961) provides a powerful way of understanding people. When I realized how effective it was, I had all four of us labeled and that helped to explain many of the family dynamics. Our social situation and circumstances may influence our behavior, but we are born with a natural personality preference that seeks its own expression. All in God's will, of course. Unfortunately, very few people discover this model, so they just muddle through life without this understanding. This is explained in the appendix A.

The ENFP type of Rosalene explained her outgoing lovable nature, her ability to organize people into teams, and her bright sunny disposition. People called her a free spirit, and she could be so because she had me to pay the bills. A longtime family friend said, "How could you not love Rosalene?" However, she scored absolutely zero on preference for thinking. She was not so good with logical reasoning and could not even keep the checkbook in order, so I had to manage our finances without her help. We divided the responsibilities with her managing inside the house and me managing the outside, except she assigned me to clean the bathrooms. I never worried about her financial responsibility as she never spent any money without consulting me even though she had the checkbook. She used the money she earned for her own personal purchases. She was the very essence of life and family for me. As one widower said in the eulogy for his wife, "I made the living, and she made the living worthwhile." Her faith was secure. She would say, "The Bible says it, I believe it, and that settles it." I often wonder what she really believed, but she did not share her deepest feelings with me.

It was not a perfect relationship. When we encountered a sensitive issue, she would say, "I don't want to talk about it." When I asked why not, she replied, "Because it upsets me." When I tried to share my workday with her, she asked, "What has that go to do with me?" So, I had to keep my work life and home life in separate compartments. One of my regrets is the lack of communications, which prevented us from really connecting deeply with each other. In the end, I was not able to penetrate her boundaries, so her death left a lot of unfinished business, which was a complicating factor in my grief. We both were introverted feelers so there were lots of thoughts in our heads that never came out of our mouths. They say love conquers all and that certainly was true for me. I never had any feelings of insecurity. In the hospital, she said, "I always loved you in my own way." And, "You are always number one."

My INTJ nature requires deep investigations into a wide range of new ideas and seeks to create order and reason among uncertainty and disorder. That is why even in retirement, I spend my days searching the Internet for any new information that I can use. A day without learning some new information is a lost opportunity for me. My reasoning ability is acute and causes difficulties in relationships when I point out the slightest faulty logic. My frustration is finding no one whom I can share it all with who can keep up with me intellectually. My personality type worked well for me in my NECA career and was a good fit, except for the need to remember names and faces of people I saw only occasionally. Unfortunately, I am a very rare type of personality, less than 3 percent of the population, and so I have very few peers who could understand my makeup without great effort. Dr. Jung complained of having the same problem of feeling isolated with no one to share his work with because it seemed to be "incomprehensible."

The MBTI explains a lot about family dynamics if you really understand it. Dr. Jung said if you don't understand someone, you tend to think they are a fool. My family members were so diverse it had more potential for disintegration than integration. My feelings about parenting were expressed by Elenore "Nelly" Custis, granddaughter of Martha Washington, in a letter she wrote to a childless married friend. Nelly buried seven children and her husband before she died. "I have often told you, my dearest friend, that you were happier in being without those precious objects of devoted affection which bind our hearts to earth, and although sources of happiness, are also sources of most heartrending anxiety and overwhelming affliction." The thing about parenting is no matter how old the kids get, you can always see the lovable child in them, and you recall carrying them around in your arms and those priceless hugs. And you can recall life in the years before they were born, but they cannot ever recall living without you. I had hoped to raise enough money to leave for their security, but the great recession of 2009 and indefinite uncertainty of the stock market thwarted my plans, so I do the best I can to preserve the savings I have. When I asked Rosalene in the hospital what she liked most about me, she replied, "You are very dependable." I had to be because she was like a kite without a tail that needed my ballast to help keep her grounded.

When I retired, there was an old folks club in my neighborhood that met monthly for potluck lunches and occasional ventures to local restaurants. It began with fifteen or more attendees, but the group gradually dwindled as one after the other died or moved away. It is no longer active, which leaves me essentially with no social support. I volunteered to help some of the widows who have died. I inspected several of the county senior citizens centers, but I felt uncomfortable seeing the people on walkers and in wheelchairs sitting around aimlessly. The food they served for lunch was not impressive either. Counting neighbors, friends, coworkers, and relatives, I have attended more than thirty-two funerals. All beginnings come with endings, and I hate that. I was a long-range planner in my occupation, and now when I look at my future, I see suffering and humiliation. Jesus told his disciple, "When you were young you dressed yourself and went wherever you pleased, but when you are old someone else will dress you and take you where you do not want to go" (John 21:18).

Loving and Losing

> "I hold it true, whate'er befall;
> I feel it, when I sorrow most;
> 'Tis better to have loved and lost
> Than never to have loved at all."
> Alfred Lord Tennyson

When Rosalene died, I was only fifty-two years old, and I had no one before her since we got married at age twenty-one. I was very naïve indeed when I got married. My father had given me no instructions about women except to say, "Keep that thing in your pants." All I knew when I got married was what I had read in a few library books and what an older neighbor kid taught me and my brother during hot summer playtimes inside a tent that my father set up. I often wonder if my parents knew what was going on. Today, you might even call that sexual abuse I suppose. My mother told me never to get married and if I did, never to have any children, but my destiny demanded I take a different pathway.

Before getting married, I had to be interviewed and instructed by the USAF base chaplain, Major Westlake, who I recall said to me, "Sergeant, I will give you the same advice I got from my father. He told me there are two things a young man should never do unless you cannot help yourself. One is to become a preacher and the other is to get married." I never thought about a career in ministry, but knew I had to marry Rosalene. That was my destiny. He referred me to a book in the library about married love, and I devoured every page. So, there I was a widower with thirteen more years to work until I could retire. Moreover, I had no memory of ever living without Rosalene in my life after thirty-one years and twenty-one days of marriage, and so I was completely bereft of any comfort or inner peace. I was like a newborn infant running around looking for someone to whom I could reconnect my umbilical cord. In short, I was a very needy man.

When I went to the church pastor, the Reverend E. E. "Duke" Wheeler, for prayer and grief counseling, he said, "I am sorry, I cannot help you." I felt betrayed and abandoned by a belief system I trusted that did not provide the solace I needed so desperately. He had his own issues with God as his oldest son was killed in an auto accident after college in the summer while scheduled to enter Harvard divinity school in the fall. He pounded the podium one Sunday morning and reprimanded the congregation for suggesting his son was with the Lord. "Don't tell me it was God's will for my son to be killed." At a deacon meeting during the last months, I could not pray because I said the die was cast and prayer was no longer helpful. Friedrich Neitzsche (1844–1900) said, "Hope is the worst of all evils for it prolongs the torments of man."

I asked our family doctor for help with my grief when I stopped by to thank him for caring for us, the one who did the mastectomy and my surgeries, and he referred me to a psychiatrist. He thanked me for stopping by because family members of his lost patients never did. He was very special and even had given me his personal home phone number. I used it once when he removed a large splinter from my finger on a Sunday afternoon. After hearing my plight, the psychiatrist said, "You are not psychotic or neurotic. I think this is situational depression, and when your situation improves, you will feel better." Like he was going to bring back my wife and protect me in my job and return my life to normal.

My son saw the distress I was in and began looking for grief counselors and books that might help me to survive because he was afraid that I would commit suicide. He sensed a very real danger because the thought did occur to me. He called the office at 9:00 a.m. every day to see if I had arrived safely. My first therapist was a married woman who hugged me on the way out, until she stopped. When I asked her why, she said, "It is time for you to ask for what you want." I never had to ask Rosalene for hugs because she always seemed to be glad to see me, so that was a totally foreign idea to me. I never did feel comfortable doing it. She recommended that I write a journal to help process my loss, and I think that project started me on the writing that merged into a dozen books. One counselor and book led me to another and another, but I thought I would die if I did not soon find another woman in my life. They say that widowers either get remarried or die, but I did neither.

The church married friends who were so close to Rosalene avoided me like I had a contagious disease, and I did. It is called post trauma shock. This reaction is driven by mirror neurons in the brain, which seem to "catch" emotions as though they are contagious, whether positive or negative. Think about football games and funerals plus the lemming-like crowd mentality that drives much of human behavior. Ideas—positive and negative—are just as contagious as emotions. Because they could see their own futures in me, they stayed clear for fear of being contaminated, and I suppose they just did not know what to do. My son explained, "They were all Mom's friends and not yours." So, I resigned my married couples Sunday school teaching position and transferred to the singles group. However, they were much younger, and I did not feel comfortable with them. One of them was a single mother named Emma aged thirty with a young son named Sean who said that she thought we would make a "nice little family." I sometimes wonder whatever happened to them, especially Sean because he was a special little boy. One younger single woman made attempts to get close to me, sitting next to me and holding my hand in church, but I was not ready for her. I left the church because I felt more pain than comfort sitting there. The religion of Rosalene had failed me completely. It was as Albert Einstein (1879–1955) said when he discovered the new laws of physics. The earth was removed from under my feet, and there was no firm place left on which to stand. I felt like an astronaut must feel floating untethered to his spaceship in the vastness of the universe. I had not thought much about the existential questions, but now the search for meaning in my life became a personal quest I could no longer ignore.

Among my reading, I found *A Grief Observed* (1963) by C. S. Lewis. He was a British theologian who married late in life, only to lose his beloved wife to breast cancer shortly after. He wrote:

> Go to Him when your need is desperate, when all other help is vain, and what do you find? A door slammed in your face and a sound of bolting and double bolting on the inside. After that silence, you might as well turn away. The longer you wait the more emphatic the silence will become. There are no lights in the windows. It might be an empty house. Why is He so present a commander in our time of prosperity and so very absent a help in our time of trouble? There is not much chance I will stop believing in God, but I fear that I will come to believe such terrible things about him. So, this is what God really is like. Deceive yourself no longer.

C. S. Lewis lost the will to live and died within two years. His story was not comforting to me, but I was glad I found another widower who suffered like I did. Where do you go when you are suffering and you realize God is causing your suffering?

Something inside me had the will to live and so I kept on going, although my coworkers feared for my survival because I lost a lot of weight and presented an ashen face to the world. My son would call the office each morning to see if I arrived safely. He encouraged me to get active socially to meet eligible women by saying, "Dad, all you have to do is show up." That was a totally foreign concept to me, but it turned out that he was right. A strange thing happened while I was buying a croissant for breakfast. A woman named Naomi asked me why I looked so badly, and when I explained my loss, she said she was a healer and maybe she could help me. I went to her house several times after work where she would put me into a semi-hypnotic sleep. I dreamed or imagined that I knew Rosalene in several previous lives. In one of them, I saved her from drowning in a river crossing while

I drowned. I have been afraid of deep water all my life. In another encounter, I was a knight on horseback, and she was a princess. I never knew what to make of that experience.

About a year after Rosalene died, I attended a week-long grief workshop conducted by the late psychiatrist, Elizabeth Kubler-Ross at Front Royal, Virginia. I watched very angry people who claimed they were abused—kneel on a mattress and beat up telephone books with a rubber hose all day, called emoting. I tried it, but it did not do anything for me. She was famous for writing a book titled *On Death and Dying* (1969) in which she observed that dying patients in nursing homes went through stages of shock, denial, anger, bargaining, and depression before entering a peaceful stage of acceptance at their pending death. She also claimed that few Americans ever properly grieve their losses, so they are walking around in a very broken state all their lives. I did not know her book existed when Rosalene died. I doubt that she would have needed it, but I could be wrong.

On the drive home, a woman attendee at the workshop named Lydle flagged me at a stoplight, which started one of my many attempts to find a replacement for Rosalene. Within a couple months, I had convinced myself she was sent to me by God, just as I thought Rosalene had been. I even bought her a ring and proposed marriage. My father-in-law had remarried after one year so I thought I could also. Lydle was the daughter of a German refugee from the post-WWII years who carried a large chip on her shoulder. She was five years older than I. After a few narrow escapes from her volatile temper, I concluded she was more burden than benefit. I left a goodbye voice mail on her phone, so I never saw her again. I am sorry that I probably hurt her. But she confirmed that I was "a very virile man" and could function again with a healthy woman, if I could only find one. Not only that, but recall I had a vasectomy at age thirty-eight, and that really made me a more desirable stud. I was not bad looking, and one woman even said I was a very handsome man. I also made sure the women all came first, several times.

The next year, I attended another grief workshop where I met a tall blonde younger woman aged thirty-eight named Louise. She was the recent widow of a US Navy officer and had a high-level government career. She invited me to her townhouse near where I lived and as I fumbled a bit, she tried to encourage me by saying, "I am giving you permission so give yourself permission." That worked, and we had a blistering affair for almost two years. Louise said that she wrote her thesis for a graduate degree in psychology comparing the lives of nuns with whores, and if she had to choose, she would pick whore. Louise said I was the best lover she ever had, but when I asked her how many lovers she had, she replied, "None of your G—business." We traveled to Philadelphia to see the Liberty Bell, to New York for the Christmas show at Radio City, to the Grand Canyon, Puerto Rica, and even to Mexico for long hot weekends. It was on the Grand Canyon trip with her that I discovered Sedona, Arizona, which provided the genesis for my new belief system. I returned several times on my business trips to the Southwest. I began writing the first book in my series, *Voices of Sedona*, while seated in the covered veranda of the restaurant at the airport in 1989.

Louise was a strong ISTJ (see appendix A) introvert whose father never understood her need for private time after school. He wanted her to socialize more, and when she refused, he broke her radio. When he was dying in a VA hospital in Nashville, she asked me to go visit him on a weekend, which I did. I asked for too much commitment from Louise and she said, "Lew, don't look a gift horse in the mouth." But I did. On a summer day after the July Fourth holiday, she bought me lunch, dropped me at the front door, and said, "Lew, I don't think we are right for each other so don't call me. I'll call you." I was somewhat relieved as I was in way over my head. She never did call me until about ten years later when we had a final good-bye lunch. She told me she had survived cancer and had canceled her career plans so she could retire early.

Following that loss, I learned there was a Unitarian church near the NECA office in Bethesda that hosted gatherings for singles on Friday nights, so I began to attend. After a brief opening with snacks, they broke up into separate rooms for various lectures and discussions. In one of them, I met Mary, who had deep brown eyes. She was a divorcee from Florida who had moved to DC to get married that was immediately annulled because her husband just ignored her. After a few months of casual dating, she relocated back to Gainesville, Florida, for family reasons and invited me to visit. I thought it might be nice to have a friend to visit in Florida so I did, and again, I got an invitation I could not refuse. We took several trips together including New York and New Orleans, where we enjoyed room service in a French Quarter hotel. As we sat on the balcony sipping mimosas in the hotel's white chenille bathrobes and listening to the calliope on the deck of a river tour boat, she said, "Oh, Lew, this is me." And, "You don't know how good that feels." Mary had a lot of potential because she loved homemaking, including baking cakes from scratch. But the distance and absenteeism became an issue, and I fell into temptation again.

The next time it occurred was when I was invited to present a grief talk to a group of widows who had read the book that I published titled *Recovery from Loss* (1990) with help of my coauthor, a psychologist and Lutheran minister who I met through the Association for Psychological Type. I used the Myers Briggs Type Indicator (MBTI), a unique model of grief based on the personality theory of Swiss psychiatrist C. G. Jung, whom I had discovered in my readings. Researching and writing the book were good therapy for me. We presented something new and different for counselors to use to help those in mourning. At the meeting of widows where I was invited to speak, there was a striking young woman only aged twenty-eight named Luz from Mexico who had emigrated to marry a gringo who died on her from colon cancer at the young age of thirty-two. After the meeting, she called me to ask, "Can you help me before I lose my mind?" Yes, I could, and I did.

Thanks to her husband's insurance, Luz was enrolled in graduate school at University of Maryland studying architecture and owned her own home. I met her parents and siblings from Mexico on several of their visits, and at one point, she said her father had told her mother that he wished we could be married. I did too, I was that far in love, or maybe it was cathexis or just sex addiction. I even took a course in Spanish. Buenos dias. Luz was an athletic person who had a basketball scholarship from the University of Mexico, so we enjoyed playing racquetball at my local gym. Our encounters were too hot to describe, but I shall never forget them. She always called it the ultimate pleasure. At one point, she asked me if I were taking something and I replied, "Only you." When I asked my therapist how long this could go on, he replied, "As long as you both want it to." She gradually got over her grief and after nearly two years, she said, "Lewsito, I don't want to be age fifty married to a man age eighty." And so that was it.

She gave me a countdown of ten days to prepare for the ending. Her loss put me into therapy again and for a time, I attended a sex anonymous group on Saturday mornings to evaluate my behavior with her. She returned a few times for dessert, but then she got married and moved on. Once again, I had a major adjustment to loss as I was totally invested in her, more likely addicted to her. With Luz, I had the highest highs and the lowest lows of my life. My boss recognized my distress and said, "Lew, perhaps you should get some counseling." If he only knew.

After a recess from relationships for several months, I went back to the Unitarian church singles parties and through several meetings there, I met three more ladies over a short period—Joanna, Janice, and Eve. These were short affairs lasting a few months each because they were impossible to sustain. Actually, I think Eve answered one of my singles ads in the *Washingtonian* magazine. She was a very big woman who was just too much for me to handle. Joanna was a divorced mother of two daughters, a community college professor, who gave me a birthday party with some friends, and who may have been the one that got away. She preferred home cooking to eating out, and she liked canoeing on the lake in my neighborhood. Janice probably was the most beautiful woman I ever met. She had been married four times and was fixing to make me the fifth because she said, "You are the nicest man I ever met." She was an interior designer who liked to party every night after work. She went out dancing at bars and drank wine until bedtime. I really tried to keep up with her, but it was just too much. After attending the annual NECA Christmas party with me, she concluded, "If you were honest with yourself, you would admit that my lifestyle is twisting you like a pretzel." And she was right.

MY RESURRECTION FROM HELL

During this phase of my life, I was in therapy with several different counselors—males and females—psychologists and a psychiatrist trying to find out who I really was and what I really wanted. My psychiatrist told me to recall the happiest time of my life and try to reconstruct that persona. I chose my senior year in high school, which was before all the troubles began to happen. He diagnosed me with dysthymia and prescribed medication, which I took for six months and then phased out because it was making me a zombie at work, and I could not continue in that condition. I also had enrolled for counseling with the graduate school clinic at George Mason University. After nearly two years of weekly sessions learning the Beck/Burns model for mental health called cognitive-behavioral therapy (CBT), I felt a lot better and more able to control my negative thinking. My counselor would challenge me to justify negative thoughts, "Is thinking like that making you feel better or worse?" However, I still missed my previous lifestyle and my wife and family. Reconstructing a new life just did not seem to be worth the effort. The real burdens were not worth the potential benefits of something new.

I was drawn back to Sedona several times alone while on business trips. After I saw the statue of the founding matriarch at the village library, Sedona Schnebly, I felt called to visit often because there was something there for me to learn that could help me recover. I arranged side visits on my business trips. In one such trip, I had a reading by a mystic psychic woman who claimed that she saw Rosalene standing at my shoulder. She said that Rosalene wanted me to have a good time, but she did not want me to get married again. That sounded much like her because near her death in the hospital, she declared, "We are still a team." When I returned from a trip, her standard greeting was, "Did you have a good time?" I can believe that she brought those several women into my life to supply the variety that she could not from her prim and proper upbringing as the preacher's daughter. Thank you, Rosalene, I think. However, I learned that hooking up was not the same as a lifelong commitment in marriage. The psychic also said Rosalene never knew how to deal with her daughter, and she still doesn't. I could believe that, for sure. That was a generational repeat because Rosalene's father did not know what to do with her either. They both were free spirits. However, Rosalene had me to pay the bills, and my daughter never married.

I stayed in the office after work and began to write. I was presented with five imaginary "teachers" who helped me write the second edition of *Voices of Sedona*. Sedona is considered by some visitors to be a very spiritual place that was occupied by the Sinagua Indians, until they left. Remnants of their village and lifestyle are preserved near there in a national park called Montezuma's Castle. It is not really a castle, and Montezuma never was there. In five metaphysical encounters, the teachers explained five principles of theofatalism that have grown now into a series of books that seem to provide the healing I so sorely needed. The books contain a series of essays connecting the principles to many different aspects of life, news, history, economics, politics, cosmology, geology, and more. I didn't really go looking for them. They just seemed to come to me through intuitive imagination. They all led me to the same conclusion that I call theofatalism. More about that in part four.

After a respite of a couple years, at the suggestion of my psychiatrist, I again placed a singles ad in the *Washingtonian* magazine around 1995, and Lisa, a divorcee with an adopted son and daughter, replied. This began my longest affair that lasted nearly six years, until she decided to end it in 2001. We took trips to New York, Sedona, Puerto Rico, and to Maine using my frequent flyer tickets. She said, "I wish we could make this permanent." She wanted me to move into her house in Bethesda, only a ten-minute drive from my office. I stayed over some nights, but I did not move. Lisa was the most accommodating woman I ever met. She liked to take showers with me and was totally uninhibited in the bedroom. She would ask me, "What can I do for you?" She was not talking about cooking or house cleaning. I found that very appealing because Rosalene was very rigid in that department. She was more liberated than I assume was her mother, but not much. I don't like to say this, but neither of us could tolerate the available birth control methods, so I was very frustrated trying to avoid making her pregnant until after I had the vasectomy. I did not want the responsibility of a large family, and I gather neither did she.

Lisa was committed to her church, which required that she must be either married or celibate to retain her role as an officer on the session or board, and she was neither. The conflict drove her to drink even more than her usual alcoholism, and then burglaries by her adopted son that got him a nine-year prison sentence really made her life miserable. In the end, she exclaimed that I was "more of the problem than the solution" since I would not marry again to preserve my meager estate for my two children. Neither did I want to ever go through again what I did after watching Rosalene die, and I did not want anyone to have to go through that with me. Unfortunately, I found out that Lisa had a recurrence of breast cancer and died on November 12, 2005, at age sixty-two. How ironic is that?

Now, it gets very dicey as something very unusual happened, what Jung might call synchronicity. I had written a book as the "readers digest" version to summarize the many books I had read on healthy relationships for cohabiting couples. I called it *Kisses Aren't Contracts*. Thinking it might be useful in college, I asked Lisa's adopted daughter which of her Tulane University professors might be interested in such a topic, and she replied, "Probably a sociology professor."

As an association executive, I thought there probably was an association for sociology professors, and I found it. Moreover, they rented out their membership list for promotions. So, I bought a random sample of a thousand names and mailed each one a brief notice about *Kisses Aren't Contracts*. It so happened that a sociology professor named Sarah at the University of Maine had recently renewed her membership after several years being inactive and received one of my notices. Was that a coincidence, or what? She liked the book after reading a copy I sent her, and she required her family-life class to buy copies. When I saw the large order, I contacted her—or did she contact me. Anyway, we connected, and she invited me to visit her class for a lecture. Of course, I could not resist any woman's invitation and I went, taking Lisa with me. I concluded in therapy that my response to the call from a woman comes from my role as my mother's helper around the house while she let my brother run off and play. That was in fall of 1999. You can probably guess the outcome.

Sarah had become the latest woman in my life. When I asked what she was thinking behind those green eyes, she replied, "Possession." After Lisa left, we bid for and got a research grant from the NECA Foundation that enabled us to spend some time alone together, officially. It is more than ironic, but the only woman who possibly could replace Rosalene in my life was securely married. For some reason, I wanted her to "know" me so she would never forget just as I would not forget. She gave me plenty of encouragement, if you know what I mean, maybe even being the aggressor. If you believe in reincarnation, perhaps it was a reunion of two souls from some past life because it felt so natural. We got to the point of discussing her divorce, but she decided for security and family she would stay with her husband, a college research professor who loved her ever since high school. She claimed she never had the feelings for him that she had for me. He did not deserve to lose his wife any more than I deserved to lose mine, and I would not want her to void the image of perfect wife and mother for her family that she is, except for this one thing. I knew it was adultery, but I could not control my behavior.

I found some self-acceptance, if not forgiveness, in knowing Apostle Paul had wrestled with his demons and lost. "I have the desire to do what is good, but I cannot carry it out. For I do not do the good I want to do, but the evil I do not want to do, this I keep on doing. What a wretched man I am." (Rom. 7:18–19, 24) He wrote this near the end of his life after organizing the incipient church of Christ. If he could not control his behavior, what chance have I? Perhaps Paul was observing in his human nature what C. G. Jung called the "shadow" side of behavior that exists in all of us. This could be the hand of God that wields Satan in the affairs of human beings described by St. Clement. For Paul, the solution was faith in the saving grace of Jesus from Nazareth.

Although Sarah confessed our very brief affair to her priest and to her husband after she converted to Catholicism, which she described as a homecoming, we still visited every Friday by email until May 2015 when I suggested it was time to end it, and she agreed. She knitted a shawl for me that I never had cleaned to preserve her energy around my shoulders, which felt like a loving hug. I wrote her husband an apology for my behavior. I am not a homewrecker. Personally, I believe there are no mistakes, just predestined choices and inevitable consequences. If you can believe that God controls everything, then remorse, regret, guilt, shame, blame, and fear have no power. Of course, this requires letting go of belief in the illusion of free will, something most Christians are not ready to do, but that must be God's will too. I shall probably never see her or hear her delightful voice again, but if Sarah ever shows up at my door, I will not send her away.

There followed another very short interlude with a divorcee named Monica that never really got started before she returned to Marblehead, Massachusetts, to take care of her aged mother. She said, "I think you just love women." After she moved away in 2002, I never tried to hook up with a woman again. At my age of seventy, it no longer seemed to be worth the effort involved in meeting strangers and getting to know them intimately. I had come to the place where I did not want anyone to know me intimately, either.

I should probably add one more incident. I was totally estranged from my brother since Thanksgiving Day 1989, when he said he would shoot me if I ever went there again. His third and bipolar wife lied and told him I had written to her that I saw him with a woman while parked in his truck in my area, for what reasons never known. I did write him a letter inviting them for dinner, but that is moot now. She claimed the letter for proof was destroyed, and he believed her. They were soon divorced, but I never went back again.

After my brother died in January 2006 from surgery for aorta repair, a friend of his named Virginia called to tell me the news. I wanted her to know a different kind of Tagliaferre, and so I invited her for several outings. We did the tours and concerts around DC and the usual lunches. I took her to the Marine Band concert, to the National Arboretum, to the Mount Vernon home of George Washington, and to a Christmas bell choir performance. It was mostly a platonic relationship as she was acquainted with my mother and father, and she said my father and her father were best friends after my absence. I say it was platonic, except for the time I visited her, and she said, "I really need you." Virginia had a lot of pent-up kundalini energy that needed to be discharged, and I was glad to help. We talked monthly by phone, so it was very painful for me when she contracted the Lou Gehrig's disease (ALS) that results in total paralysis. I visited her a few days before she died in October 2012 while in hospice, cared for by her doting daughter, wasted to less than a hundred pounds and barely able to speak. She was a nice lady who never deserved the troubled life that she had. Her bisexual husband died at age fifty-eight, and several men misused her afterward. God has a lot of explaining to do. I did not expect that I would miss her so much. There was yet another blow still to come.

Some things get hardwired into memory that cannot be forgotten. Here are some comments I recall from my several affairs that remain stuck in my mind. I like to think Rosalene had something to do with sending the women to me because she always wanted me to have a good time, but not to get married again. I always went only where I was invited, and I never stayed where I was not wanted. The memories are bitter/sweet.

    Jean said, "Oh, Lewy, I should have waited for you."
    Rosalene said, "I always loved you in my own way."
    Lydle said, "You are a very virile man."
    Louise said, "You are the best lover I ever had."
    Mary said, "You don't know how good that feels."
    Luz said, "Te amo con todo mi corazon."
    Joanna said, "I am going to tie you to the bed post."
    Janice said, "Happy birthday."
    Eve said, "You could get into trouble."
    Lisa said, "I wish we could make this permanent."
    Sarah said, "Yes, do it, do it, do it…"
    Monica said, "I think you just love women."
    Virginia said, "I really need you."

MY RESURRECTION FROM HELL

I was never very close to Rosalene's brother, but his wife was always nice to me. She gave up her career in nursing to manage their radio station and helped to make them successful. She had double mastectomies over several years and then developed spinal cancer. I visited her a few days before her death on November 3, 2014, from a terminal stroke, which made her left side totally paralyzed. I thought her death merely was another passing loss, but I was cast into major depression as a delayed reaction about six months later. Her death triggered renewal of the memories and grief after losing Rosalene and all the others. When you add up my many losses and disappointments, it is a wonder I am still here. On the Holmes-Rahe scale of stress, I am off the chart. After each loss, I felt like one of those children's toys that keeps bouncing back up whenever it is knocked over. Or maybe like the phoenix rising from ashes over and over. More often, I felt like Humpty-Dumpty who fell off a wall and could not be put back together again. Or like I was carrying a mountain gorilla around on my back. God really knows how to test a person.

There is an end to every rope, and I came dangerously close to mine. Several times, I thought I would be better off dead. Sometimes, God gives people more burdens than they can carry. Call it despair, the complete loss of hope, and the depletion of resilience. When I looked to scripture for relief, I found this. Jesus said, "Take my yoke upon you and learn from me, for I am gentle and humble in heart, and you will find rest for your souls. For my yoke is easy and my burden is light" (Matt. 11:29–30). I think he lied. Jesus did not protect all those Christian martyrs who died because of him, killed by lions in the arena, and beheaded and crucified for inciting insurrection, or refusing to worship pagan gods of Rome. Persecution of Christians did not end until Emperor Constantine was converted about the year 325 CE. But, hey, Jesus said, "The spirit gives life, the flesh counts for nothing" (John 6:63). And that settles it. *Not*. Jesus promised his disciples eternal life, but they had to give up theirs to get it. "If anyone comes to me and does not hate father and mother, wife and children, brothers and sisters—yes, even their own life—such a person cannot be my disciple (Luke 14:26–33). I just know too much.

One more thing. I read where it is a good idea for older people living alone to have a pet, so I decided to look for a dog in 2003. I searched on the Internet and saw the picture of a cute white puppy with a black eye and black ears. There were many dogs at the kennel, but she came running out of the pack straight to me. For nearly fifteen years, EllieBird was my faithful companion. She made the otherwise dead house come alive with her presence. She was the perfect dog and maybe the perfect roommate for me. She was always happy to see me come home. So was Rosalene. Perhaps the hardest decision I ever made, after choosing not to put Rosalene on life support, was taking EllieBird to the vet for the last time at 6:30 p.m. on May 18, 2018. I knew that all beginnings come with endings, but her loss seemed to cap all the others. I probably cried more for her than all the other losses combined. I know all beginnings come with endings, but it seems like God sometimes overdoes it.

Once again, the house seemed dead inside with nothing moving so I kept the television set on to fake company. I felt the rush of grief flooding my soul again. I reentered therapy with counselors at my medical provider and consulted a psychiatrist for medication. They suggested that I write a journal about my life with EllieBird, and so I did. I don't know if dogs have a soul or not, but I know EllieBird definitely had a personality, which suited me perfectly. Sometimes, I can still feel her presence close by me.

In 2010, I had four surgical procedures in my left eye to correct retinal tears, macular peels, and cataracts that threatened my sight. I developed the common male aging symptoms of benign prostate hypertrophy, which twice required me to wear a catheter during acute urinary tract infections. I can tell you that is not fun. I was scheduled for surgery, but I managed to defer it by experimenting with diet supplements after the prescription drugs came with intolerable side effects.

That medical crisis effectively ended my career as well as my sex life because I became totally impotent after it. Otherwise, my physical condition remained good for a man my age, but I had to work constantly on my mental health. I gained more weight than I like, but when eating is the only pleasure you have left, guess what.

When I look back, I think my lifeline to sanity was writing those several books. And it is with this one, too. I took in as much information as I could from cable TV education channels, Wikipedia, and other online sources. As I learned more about how the world that God made really works, I was compelled to report on the new belief system I was given to accommodate my life and losses. More about that in part four.

After my daughter was diagnosed with mental illness in 2003, I attended family training and support groups with the National Alliance on Mental Illness (NAMI). These connections expanded my awareness of all the suffering souls in the world who did not volunteer for this "new normal." However, I think that all burdens come with benefits if you can find them. With every loss, something also is gained; the negative is needed to make the positive work. I have learned and developed a new compassion for people with disabled family members and for the disabled themselves. There really are only three options about suffering: (1) God wants to prevent it, but he cannot. (2) God could prevent it, but he chooses not to. (3) God is causing the suffering. It is hard to worship a loving God after you learn that God is causing the suffering. Depression and anxiety may be reasonable reactions, also fear and anger. I had to deal with all of them. Life goes on and as Rosalene said, "Please be patient because God is not finished with me yet."

PART III

Lessons Learned

I have learned a lot since the loss of Rosalene. Much of it goes beyond the traditional belief we lived with that I think probably never would have occurred had she been healthy and continued to live. As with most married people, we probably would have continued in the lifestyle we had been living. She had a "bucket list" she wanted to complete after the kids were gone, which included visiting the national parks and all the state capitals. She also liked historically covered bridges. We got to visit a few of them, but her list was far from completed. She never bemoaned her untimely illness so I can only imagine how she felt having her life prematurely ended with her goals unfinished. When I asked her how the day went, she replied, "I had a brief pity party but it has passed." Since her death, my growth has been broadened into directions I never could have imagined and in ways in which I did not intentionally seek. In the following sections, I will discuss four of the survival skills I learned after she died that would have made living with Rosalene so very much better. These sections are based on dialectical behavior therapy (DBT), developed by Dr. Marsha Linehan and other online sources. I am writing them in a different voice as lessons learned, hoping that some readers who are suffering a major loss might find them helpful. The goal of DBT is to achieve a life that is worth living in terms of your own values and beliefs. I spent hundreds of hours and thousands of dollars in therapy learning these skills so perhaps they will save you some serious money. Time and practice are required to learn them. I still must work on them constantly to avoid slipping back into old behaviors.

Mindful Living

In recent years, the practice of meditation has migrated from eastern traditions to the West Coast and then across the country. C. G. Jung said, "The one who looks outward dreams. The one who looks inward awakes." I described above that people have the uncanny ability to imagine things unseen, and this can cause them pain as well as pleasure. A solution to the painful part that is emerging is to shut off imagination to concentrate on the here and now. Since the past is only a memory and the future is unknown, focusing energy on the senses can help to reduce suffering caused by grief, remorse, anxiety, and fear. The applications of mindfulness meditation are well established; however, the mechanisms that underlie this practice are yet to be fully understood. Some research suggests that practicing meditation may reduce blood pressure, symptoms of irritable bowel syndrome, anxiety and depression, and insomnia. It also is a proven way of accepting life as it is. One example is "decentering," a focus on becoming aware of all incoming thoughts and feelings and accepting them, but not attaching or reacting to them.

The Buddhist solution to suffering is contentment. Apostle Paul said the same thing, more or less.

> I have learned to be content in whatever situation I am in. I know how to be humble, and I know how to prosper. In each and every situation, I have learned the secret of being full and of going hungry, of having too much and of having too little. (Phil. 4:11–12)

In contrast, American capitalism is driven by discontent, and the economy is driven by converting luxuries into necessities. For example, I am old enough to remember cars came without air conditioning, power brakes and power steering with manual cranks on the door windows, radios contained vacuum tubes you could replace at a drug store, and party line telephones were normal, if you could afford one. Hence, this concept may be foreign to many younger readers, but read on. It may be helpful.

The introduction to mindfulness in dialectical behavior therapy (DBT) by Dr. Marsha Linehan states:

> These skills are central to DBT. They teach how to observe and experience reality as it is, to be less judgmental, and to live in the moment with serenity and inner peace. DBT mindfulness skills are translations of meditation practices from eastern and western traditions into specific behaviors you can practice. No religious convictions are expected or necessary for practicing these skills. They focus on balancing two opposing polarities: working to achieve goals while at the same time letting go of attachment to achieving goals—hence the dialectical. Many things can cause us pain but our options for response are limited. We can solve the problem causing pain, we can try to feel better by changing our response, we can accept and tolerate the problem and our response, or we can stay miserable and possibly make it worse.

Contemporary mindfulness began when biologist emeritus, Jon Kabat-Zinn had a "vision" during a meditation retreat in 1979. It prompted him to start a meditation-based program for stress and chronic pain at the University of Massachusetts Medical School, where he worked. This was the precursor of Mindfulness Based Stress Reduction (MBSR), a widely used, eight-week intervention that includes techniques such as mindfulness of breathing and walking meditation, drawn largely from traditional Buddhist practice. This in turn has produced Mindfulness Based Cognitive Therapy (MBCT)

MY RESURRECTION FROM HELL

for depression and Mindfulness Based Relapse Prevention (MBRP) for addictive behaviors. Mindfulness now is being used in business, education, and the military to help improve individual performance and to reduce stress. I think it is very effective in grief management also.

When you are submerged under the powerful challenges of grief, it is easy to lose your serenity. Dr. Linehan says we must absorb some misery to get out of hell. This is much healthier than self-medicating with drugs, alcohol, and food or dangerous behavior. Much research during the past few decades has affirmed that mindful living is good for you, and it may be good for the planet too.

If we cannot find some resilience for stressful situations that seem to have no way out, we can sink into depression and let anxiety rule. In that condition, the mind shifts into endless ruminations, which lead nowhere, like wandering around in a maze with apparently no way out. Ruminations concentrate thoughts on the past and the future, neither of which we can control. It is like a car stuck in mud or snow, only drilling deeper into the muck the more it spins its wheels. Many troubled people are so engaged in spinning their wheels. They cannot take time out to gain any traction. In contrast, mindful living focuses on experience of the here and now, without judging and with acceptance of reality as it is. That is the place of inner peace. This is not like sitting on a pillow and repeating some single-syllable mantra as in Buddhist meditation. It is more like a car with traction control that can concentrate power on the wheel that has the most grip. It is an approach to life, you can practice wherever you are and whatever you are doing. In fact, you must if it is to be effective. Halfway measures will not work.

For most meditators, goals for mindful living are to reduce suffering, increase contentment, and retain control of the mind—whatever that is. It is based in experiencing reality as it is in the here and now. Life comes with many things we cannot control. Plans don't work out, people disappoint, painful stuff happens, beginnings come with endings, and the future is uncertain. As we age, losses of loved ones become more common. First century Stoic philosopher Epictetus taught, "Remind yourself that whoever you love is mortal and not your own. It is given only for the present, not irrevocably nor forever, even as a fig or a bunch of grapes in the appointed season." People rarely think about endings at the beginning; if they contemplated endings at the beginnings, perhaps there would be fewer beginnings. We tend to live as though "do this, get that" will always be true so when life doesn't work that way, we can be shocked and disoriented. Living in the past invites depression, living in the future invites anxiety, and living here and now invites inner peace. The sage might say, "Don't cross the bridge before you come to it." During his last few years, my father, who was brought to America from Italy at his age of fourteen, said, "Well, Lewis, in life, we don't always get what we like so we have to be satisfied with what we get. I think I did the best I could under the circumstances." I hope I can leave the planet with the same attitude.

This outlook is important because the older you get, the more painful memories pile up and the shorter and more uncertain your future becomes. If we are to create inner peace and serenity, we must live in the here and now, moment by moment, between a past that is gone and a future that only exists in imagination. For me, that is the goal of mindful living. It evokes the merger of human doing and human being, of thinking and feeling to achieve walking the middle way. But it takes practice, practice, practice because the mind keeps slipping back into its old habits, especially under the stress of loss.

The necessary opposites require that here and now living needs to be balanced with planning for the future as it will not take care of itself. Someone said live like you may die tomorrow but plan like you might live forever. Failing to plan is planning to fail. Since we know the future is indefinitely uncertain, we must live with a certain amount of anxiety in my opinion.

The average human mind, whatever that is, is like a monkey flipping all about, now here, now there, now up, now down, etc. It is called monkey mind in eastern traditions. As such, it is like a runaway kite without a tail, swooping about with every shift of the wind. It is exhausting. In such a condition, it is like the heart that is out of sync and cannot function normally. Such a heart may be regulated with a defibrillator, but the mind is more difficult to reign in.

Using the analogy of a computer, the brain may be the hardware and the mind may be the software. Neurology researchers have discovered a lot about the hardware of the brain, but they still know very little about the software. They also have no fully developed theory of the apparent command and control function that tells the brain what to do. In mindful living, it is the software that needs changing. To achieve its full potential, the mind must be focused narrowly on one thing at a time attentively and intensely, like a laser beam. Developing this skill is a lifelong process of self-development. Since the progress is slow and subtle, you must be patient and persistent throughout the years to get the benefits of mindful living. It may be seen as a spiritual evolution. Apostle Paul related his experience this way, "Though outwardly we are wasting away, yet inwardly we are being renewed day by day" (2 Cor. 4:16). Perhaps he practiced mindful living.

As I see it, mindful living concentrates on the here and now instead of ruminating about the past or the future. H. L. Mencken (1880–1956) wrote: "We are here, and it is now. Further than that, all human knowledge is moonshine." So, when I feel anxious and want to experience inner peace, I repeat this mantra: "I am here and now." It works to calm me down and helps to create serenity in the midst of chaos which is life. Many Christians are so busy doing things and talking on their cell phones they do not take enough time for personal contemplation and spiritual nurture. Whether from Buddhism or psychology, evidence indicates that spending time each day in quiet meditation is good for you. One can learn to live in a mindfulness mode, concentrating on the here and now, because that really is all we have for sure.

In mindful living, the mind cannot drift off into ruminating about the past or the future or jumping to conclusions. It is like putting a tail on the kite, enabling it to soar on the wind without crashing. Being unburdened by intuitions, thoughts, and feelings or stressful losses, the mind can idle and let the world go by, so to speak. When in that mode, the whole body can feel relaxed, stress can be reduced, and energy can be conserved instead of being expended in useless attempts to change the unchangeable.

An anonymous patient wrote to Dr. C. G. Jung, "By keeping quiet, repressing nothing, remaining attentive, and by accepting reality, taking things are they are and not as I want them to be, by doing all this unusual knowledge has come to me and unusual powers as well. I always thought if we accepted things, they overpowered us in some way or another, but this turns out to be untrue. So, now I intend to play the game of life, being receptive to whatever comes to me, also accepting my own nature with its positive and negative sides. Thus, everything becomes more alive to me." That is what is meant by radical acceptance of reality as it is—reconciling freedom with surrender. You don't have to like your role in life, only accept it. Like gravity, if you cannot change it, you must live with it. People lived with gravity long before they understood it, but now it is a servant of mankind. It may be similar with mindful living. If mindful living becomes a way of life, the crises in losses may be navigated and managed more effectively and serenely. Since progress is slow, it requires a measure of faith to stick with it for the long haul.

As they say, "Rome was not made in a day," so it will take time and work to change life-long habits if they resist being replaced with mindfulness. Practice may begin with simple exercises and move gradually into the more complex. DBT recommends the "raisin exercise" to begin. It works like this: Put a raisin in the palm of your hand. Focus on nothing but that raisin. Look at it carefully, observing its color, texture, size, etc. Notice how it feels. Smell it and touch it with your fingers. Put the raisin in your mouth and taste it, roll it around and let it merge with the saliva that begins the process of digestion. Chew the raisin completely and swallow it, feeling it going down the esophagus until it disappears.

This raisin exercise illustrates three main aspects of mindfulness—observe, describe, participate. DBT says: Notice the sensations through your eyes, ears, nose, and tongue. Pay total attention in the moment. Focus your attention on your breathing. Push away nothing, cling to nothing. Watch thoughts come into your awareness and let them slip right by like clouds in the sky or objects floating down the river. You did not create them, and you cannot control them. Notice each feeling rising and falling like waves in the ocean. Express the experience in words to yourself. I feel sadness now. My stomach muscles are tight. I don't really like this. Focus just on the facts of the experience, not anything else, no opinions, no judgments. This raisin sure is dried up. I don't really like raisins. Throw yourself into the present moment, whatever you are doing. Transfer thoughts from self to sensations; what you see, smell, touch, taste, hear. Separate each of your senses and focus on them one at a time. Observe sights, observe sounds, observe smells, observe tastes, observe touches, observe your breathing in and out, in and out.

I bought some essential oils that I dab under my nose and dispense with a diffuser for smells that temporarily absorb my attention. My faves are magnolia, lilac, honeysuckle, and gardenia. For taste, I get a key lime pie or cheese blintz or eat a fresh peach or strawberry or some peanut butter with a banana or make some pancakes with diet syrup. For hearing, I tune in "Easy Listening" channel on cable or dial up some marching bands or Chet Atkins guitar or Arthur Rubenstein piano on YouTube or play a CD of my favorite 1950s music. Also, I enjoy watching foreign television where I can learn about the world without leaving my chair. I also explore the world on Google Earth and watch the Science and NatGeo channels on cable. For touch, I still have some work to do since my dog is gone. Sometimes, I stop typing and rub the mouse pad. For sight, I visit a park or look up at the clouds and view earth scenes on my computer on *The World from Above* and *Google Earth*. Also, I find that my attention is concentrated here and now when I try to eat with chopsticks.

The trick is to expand this simple exercise into everything that you experience—including your breathing—and do it, 24/7. Just be still for a while and pay attention to your breath, in and out, in and out. Whatever you do and where ever you are, be mindful. You can practice while making coffee, eating lunch, you can practice while washing dishes or doing the laundry, you can practice while cleaning house, you can practice while taking a bath or shower, brushing your teeth, mowing the lawn, painting a room, putting gas in the car, but not while driving. This caution brings up one important caveat.

In western cultures, people are used to doing several things at once, what is called time-sharing. The most visible example is people talking on a cell phone while doing something else—walking the dog, eating, shopping, etc. You can see people eating while texting. What you may not see is a man planning his weekend golf game during a business meeting, or a woman planning dinner while watching television. I know, this is sexist, but you can reverse the genders. The human mind is designed to do only one thing at a time. When you ask it to do two or more things at a time, it shifts rapidly from one to the other and back again. This may be where engineers got the idea for packet switching of information transfer on the Internet. If the brain must function in the time-share mode continuously, it can become fatigued and begin to slow down, like a computer that is overloaded. If more demands are made on it, mistakes begin to appear. And eventually, the brain begins to exhibit signs of stress. These reactions can include fits of temper and confusion as the brain asks for some relief. DBT says mindful living is the solution. Here is more.

Mindful living includes accepting ourselves with compassion in the moment here and now. I find this is getting more difficult as I get older, not easier, because there is more personal history to contemplate. Scripture says we must love our neighbor as ourselves. All the other commandments can be summed up in that one (Rom. 13:8–10). If that is so, then we cannot love others until we first love ourselves because we cannot give what we do not have. Conversely, by loving others, we also love ourselves. Research now is showing this ancient wisdom to be true. Feeling loved unconditionally by even one person is a healing experience. If you are not near the one you love, love the one who is near. DBT emphasizes practicing loving-kindness as a wise-mind experience from a spiritual perspective. Loving-kindness is a practice designed to increase love and compassion, first for ourselves and then for loved ones needing our care and those we are angry with and graduating up to all beings. DBT says loving-kindness can protect us from developing and holding onto judgments, ill will, and hostile feelings toward ourselves and others. We don't need to carry anymore baggage than necessary. The sage must travel light. When you think hatred and hostility, your body generates harmful, unhealthy energy. When you say a prayer for self and others, you actively express good will and produce good, healing energy.

Metta, or loving-kindness meditation, is a practice of developing positive feelings, first toward yourself and then toward others. Metta increases positivity, empathy, and compassionate behavior toward others. Take a comfortable position and hold your hands upward and open, ready to receive. Begin reciting warm loving wishes to yourself, "May I be happy. May I be at peace. May I be safe." Repeat. Gradually work up to loved ones, friends, and other caregivers. "May John/Mary be comfortable. May John/Mary be at peace. May John/Mary be happy." Eventually, you may work up to sending warm loving-kindness to all sentient beings. Peace and goodwill to all. Jesus commanded to love your enemies and do good to those who harm you (Matt. 5:43–44). However, someone said, "I don't like the people I love." We may choose our friends, but we cannot choose our families. That is okay because human beings are made to seek self-preservation first, and you cannot choose your caregiving family. Self-defense is accepted by courts of law. But you can't go around attacking people you don't like, verbally or otherwise. If you need to "blow off steam," curse and scream as you beat up a pillow. In private, of course. Take a shower or walk in nature or find some other distraction for the moment. A little escapism is okay for relief of tensions and detoxing the spirit provided you do it mindfully.

One of the western applications of mindfulness living is incorporated in acceptance commitment therapy (ACT). This approach to managing—not merely tolerating—symptoms of troubling situations was developed in the 1980s by Dr. Stephen C. Hayes, PhD, and has been promoted by Dr. Russell Harris, MD, of Australia. ACT is based on the assumption that if you think the way you want to be, you will eventually act the way you think; and if you act the way you want to be eventually you will be the way you act. The question is who or what is the *you* that makes these decisions. That is the realm of neurology or metaphysics and is yet to be determined. This assumption has some basis in scripture as follows: "Whatever you ask for in prayer, believe that you have received it, and it will be yours. If you believe, you will receive whatever you ask for in prayer" (Matt. 21:18–22, Mark 11:24). However, this declaration was directed to the disciples of Jesus and may not apply as a generality.

Some experts think ACT is the best of all worlds because it does not try to eliminate stressful events or to mask the symptoms with medications. Trying to control the uncontrollable merely increases suffering while reconciling freedom and surrender reduces it. It is not about whitewashing the troubling impact of real-world problems. ACT does not attempt to change or stop unwanted thoughts or feelings, but it encourages people to develop a different and compassionate relationship with those experiences. ACT is not about fighting your pain; it's about developing a willingness to embrace every experience life has to offer, to absorb them, and to transform them. It's not about resisting your emotions; it's about feeling them completely and yet not turning your choices over to them. Instead, we accept a natural level of physical and emotional discomfort we are in by mindfully observing what is happening, accepting it and transforming it into the best life we can have, considering all the circumstances. In ACT, this is called clean discomfort.

There's no avoiding discomfort in some stressful situations. Life serves it up to all of us in one way or another. However, once we start struggling with it, our discomfort levels increase rapidly. This additional suffering is called dirty discomfort. Our "struggle switch" is like an emotional amplifier—switch it on, and we can have anger about our anxiety, anxiety about our anger, depression about our depression, or guilt about our guilt and grief about our grief. Instead of trying to change the situation or our normal human reaction to it, ACT develops ways of accepting an uncontrollable problem and our reaction to it and moving on without doing more damage to ourselves and to others. It may be necessary to accept there are no confident solutions to some problems, only indefinite uncertainty. Sometimes, anticipating a crisis can be as stressful as the event itself. As Dr. Linehan said, we must accept misery to get out of hell. The pain of doing it is less than the pain of not doing it.

MY RESURRECTION FROM HELL

ACT relies upon six core principles as follows:

1. *Cognitive defusion.* Learning to perceive thoughts, images, memories and other cognitions as what they are—nothing more than transient bits of language, words and pictures—as opposed to what they can appear to be—threatening events, rules that must be obeyed, objective truths and facts. A thought is just a thought and not reality.
2. *Acceptance.* Making room for unpleasant feelings, sensations, urges, and other stressful experiences; allowing them to come and go without struggling with them, running from them, or giving them undue attention.
3. *Contact* with the present moment: bringing full awareness to you're here-and-now experience, with openness, interest, and receptiveness; focusing on, and engaging fully in whatever you are doing.
4. *The observing self.* Accessing a transcendent sense of self; a continuity of consciousness that is unchanging, ever-present, and impervious to harm. Imagine sitting in the back of a theater seeing yourself sitting in the front row watching a movie of your life. From this perspective, it is possible to experience directly that "you" are not your thoughts, feelings, memories, urges, sensations, images, roles, or even a physical body. These phenomena change constantly and are peripheral aspects of you, but they are not the essence of who "you" are.
5. *Values.* Clarifying what is most important, deep in your heart; what sort of person you want to be; what is significant and meaningful to you; and what you want to stand for in this life.
6. *Committed action.* Setting goals, guided by your values, and taking effective action to achieve them. It is not only about getting rid of bad feelings or getting over old trauma. It also is about creating a rich, full and meaningful life while doing what you have to do. (www.actmindfully.com.au)

I do not think this skill means neglecting planning for things needing attention in the future. Maturity includes balancing the benefits of mindful living with making plans about anticipated future issues. Anxiety about the uncertain or threatening future could be a signal to consider options and make decisions based on rational evaluation about the benefits and burdens, pros and cons. Refer to appendix B. Obviously, if you are caught in a very stressful situation, concentrating on the here and now may produce more burdens than benefits, making you want to just run away. In such a situation, you may need to invoke the emotions regulations and distress tolerance skills in the DBT inventory described in the following sections. Like any skill, knowing which tool should be used is important to the results obtained.

Now for some homework: Go off someplace by yourself and do the raisin exercise several times each day. If you cannot get some raisins, use a similar food like grapes or nuts or popcorn. Try eating with chopsticks. Select some routine activities around the house or workplace and begin extending the practice of mindfulness to them. Like, I see there is dust on my TV table. Set up a calendar and post a record of your performance. Also, work on the prayer meditation, first extending love to yourself and then to others, including the ones you love and care for. Notice your tendency to be judgmental about things or people, and consciously let go and practice accepting things as they are. Reconcile freedom with surrender. Whatever the problem is, you did not cause it and you cannot fix it—that is up to God.

Although it is a traditional practice in eastern cultures, mindful living is becoming an accepted professional practice in western therapy to help troubled people of all ages. Researchers in neurology are investigating how it works to change the wiring in the brain to improve and expand the joys of living while minimizing the impacts of stress and suffering. Pain in life may be inevitable, but suffering is optional. For more information, visit www.mindful.org

Emotions Regulation

Emotions are a necessary need of humans. Neurology researchers think emotions were some of the earliest functions developed by the primitive human brain because they were necessary for basic survival. Emotions can surge as a flood during a crisis with a mix of negative and positive reactions. They help us to communicate when words are insufficient. Feelings of love and compassion can be mixed up with fear and anger. They can be disabling if they are intense enough. They also can cause trouble if they are not regulated. Emotions are beneficial when babies need to express their needs before they can talk. You can tell if they are happy, sad, hungry, comfortable or wet by their body language. There is nothing more delightful than a happy baby, or more dismal than an unhappy one, especially in an airplane. Thus, emotions are a useful aid to communicating human needs.

Normally, emotions begin, rise, peak, and then fall. If you could move outside yourself, you could see them pass through like a summer thunderstorm. People with extraverted feeling personalities are more comfortable expressing emotions than are people with introverted feelings. Emotions can result from both positive and negative events. There are no good or bad emotions—although they can be classified negative and positive—but they can be troublesome if not kept within useful bounds while you are striving to achieve healthy aging. Everything comes with burdens and benefits, including emotions, so learning to regulate them surely is a beneficial skill to learn if you want to create serenity in the chaos of life.

In eastern traditions, emotions are integrated with life and become a normal part of human nature without question. Some of these traditions are evident on the West Coast of the USA and can be found in social and academic circles. Unfortunately, people in western cultures often are taught at an early age to stifle their emotions and to hide their feelings, or to hurry them through to get back to "normal." However, when emotions—also called affects or feelings—boil over or exceed healthy boundaries, they can do more harm than good. When they are bottled up, emotions can explode with negative consequences. Then people can feel badly about feeling badly, especially when they hurt someone they love. They call that secondary emotions. When emotions are successfully regulated, relationships go better, and when they aren't, they don't. When you are in the grip of emotions, you cannot reason effectively, and your resilience is diminished. These are some of the necessary and sufficient reasons why emotions regulation is included in dialectical behavior therapy (DBT) and why I think all readers should complete this lesson whether you are widowed or not.

Emotions are complex. They are so complex there is no generally accepted definition among scholars of different disciplines. According to some theories, they are states of feeling that result in physical and psychological changes that influence our behavior. The physiology of emotion is closely linked to arousal of the nervous system with various states and strengths of arousal relating to particular emotions. Emotions also are linked to behavioral tendency to react automatically to life-threatening challenges without having to think about it. Extraverted feeling people are more likely to be social and express their emotions, while introverted feeling people are more likely to be more socially withdrawn and conceal their emotions. Emotions often are the driving force behind motivation, positive or negative. According to other theories, emotions are not causal forces but simply reactive syndromes of various components, which might include motivation, feeling, behavior, and physiological changes.

Research on emotions has increased significantly over the past two decades with many fields contributing including psychology, neuroscience, endocrinology, medicine, history, sociology, and computer science. The numerous theories that attempt to explain the origin, neurobiology, experience, and function of emotions have only fostered more intense research on this topic. In addition, PET scans and fMRI scans help researchers study the affective processes in the brain. Emotions are not just generated from one part of our brain but rely on several interwoven networks involving the amygdala, ventral tegmental area, orbitofrontal cortex, and many more which all serve to appraise external stimuli, generate an initial emotional response, and then regulate that response as needed. A disruption in this system can lead to lack of emotions or too much, depending on the nature and location of the disturbance. The research still is primitive because exploring the living brain is like mapping the moon with a telescope.

An important aspect of emotions regulation is understanding that negative emotions are normally not dangerous, or something that must be avoided. They are a normal part of life, like weeds in a garden, but there are ways to acknowledge and then let go of these feelings so that one is not controlled by them. Often, people with extreme emotional sensitivity go through cycles that begin with an event that triggers automatic negative thoughts. These thoughts then prompt an extreme or adverse emotional response, which may subsequently lead to destructive behavioral choices. The detrimental behavior is then followed by more negative emotions, such as shame and guilt, and the cycle repeats if there is no intervention (Wikipedia).

Understanding and Labeling Emotions

The first skill in emotions regulation involves recognizing and naming emotions. In DBT, people are taught to use descriptive labels such as "frustrated" or "anxious," rather than general terms like "feeling bad," because vaguely defined feelings are much more difficult to manage. DBT recognizes and discusses the following emotions: anger, anxiety, disgust, envy, fear, jealousy, happiness, love, sadness, and shame. With each of these emotions, it describes associated words, events that prompt the emotion, interpretation of the events, associated biological changes and experiences, expressions and actions of the emotion, and aftereffects of the emotion.

An important distinction is that of primary and secondary emotions. A primary emotion is the initial reaction to an event or a triggers in one's environment, while a secondary emotion is a reaction to one's thoughts, i.e., feeling depressed about having gotten angry. Secondary emotions are emotions about emotions. They are destructive, making a person more vulnerable to unhealthy behaviors. Therefore, in addition to naming both primary and secondary emotions, it is important for elders to accept their primary emotion without judging themselves for experiencing it.

DBT skills also discuss myths about emotions, such as the misconception that there are "right" and "wrong" ways to feel in aging situations. An additional topic is the purpose that emotions serve—which is to alert us that something in our environment is either beneficial or problematic. These emotional responses are stored in memory, and we are then more prepared when encountering similar situations in the future. Additionally, our emotions communicate messages to others through our words, facial expressions, and body language—just like babies. There are three sets of emotion regulation skills in DBT, described with an acronym.

Reducing Emotional Vulnerability

The acronym for the first skill set in reducing emotional vulnerability is PLEASE MASTER.

- PL—represents taking care of our *physical health* and treating pain and/or illness.
- E—is for *eating* a balanced diet and avoiding excess sugar, fat, and caffeine.
- A—stands for *avoiding* mood-altering stuff like alcohol and drugs, which only exacerbate emotional instability.
- S—represents getting regular and adequate *sleep*.
- E—is for getting regular *exercise*.
- MASTER—refers to doing daily activities that build confidence and competency in line with your personality preference. This skill is designed to reduce emotional vulnerability. It is the building of positive experiences to balance life's negative incidents and feelings. To accomplish this goal, people are encouraged to plan

one or more daily experiences that they can look forward to and enjoy. This might be participating in a hobby or sport, reading a book, spending time with a friend, or anything that brings the individual contentment and self-esteem outside of the aging role. It is important to engage in these activities mindfully, centering attention on what one is currently doing. My son is very good with home repairs and custom carpentry. My daughter has developed expertise in assembling jigsaw puzzles, which occupies her attention to reduce anxiety from inability to control her bipolar moods. I research topics of interest on the Internet, write journals and books. If an individual has difficulty focusing on the activity, he or she is advised to try something different. The person also is encouraged to set long-term goals that will bring increased positive experiences into his or her life, such as learning a new skill or making a job change regardless of age. (*Caution: Go easy on that last one. Making a major change late in life when you are distraught can be problematic.*)

Taking opposite action means to engage in behaviors that would be typical when one is experiencing the emotion that is in direct contrast to the current feeling. For example, if you are feeling sad, you might try being active, standing straight, smile and speaking confidently—whatever you would do if happy. When you are experiencing anger, you behave as if you were calm instead; by speaking in a soft voice and doing something nice for someone. If you feel anxious about the future, focus on being totally in the here and now as in mindful living. This skill is not aimed at denying the current emotion; you should still name the emotion and absorb it, then let it go. However, acting opposite possibly will lessen the length and severity of the negative feelings. If you practice enough, these skills empower elders to regulate their emotions rather than being driven by them.

Decreasing Emotional Suffering

The last component on decreasing emotional suffering is comprised of two skills: (1) experiencing or absorbing and (2) letting go after taking opposite action. *Experiencing* is noting the emotion and observing its affect, like watching a leaf floating by on a stream or clouds floating by in the sky. Like martial arts, this skill involves absorbing the impact of strong emotions by letting them flow through and pass on by. *Letting go* refers to being aware of the current emotion through mindfulness, naming it, and then letting it go—rather than avoiding, dwelling on, or fighting it. This might involve taking a deep breath and visualizing the thought or feeling floating away or picturing the emotion as a wave that comes and goes. Imagine the emotion as a balloon and release it to float off into the sky. Emotions are time limited and will fade under normal circumstances if they are not invited to stay or are empowered by cultivating them.

Soon after our marriage, Rosalene got mad at me for some reason. When I asked her what I should do, she replied, "Just take me in your arms and I will melt." Sorry to say, that did not always work. I had to accept that she would be angry sometimes and not to take it personally. Since she was an introverted feeler, many issues went unresolved because she was not comfortable talking about them. People with introverted feelings may not, cannot, openly display their feelings and may feel them intensely until they explode. If you are on the receiving end, it is best not to respond in kind, but to let the situation cool down before engaging in any response. Just say, "Since it seems like you are feeling stressed right now, we can wait until later to discuss this when you are in a better mood." People with extraverted feelings are much more likely to express them openly, not expecting them to be fixed, just observed and acknowledged.

The emotion called worry deserves some special discussion. Worry is a natural response to anticipated future concerns, which you cannot control., i.e., loss of freedom. It is kin to anxiety with some additional complications. Worry has some benefits if it prompts actions to prevent problems—like wearing your seat belt, saving money or losing weight, getting a flu shot or buying life insurance—and reminding yourself to take your meds or drive to a medical appointment. Most of the time, worries come and go like other emotions, but they can become chronic if allowed to stay. Chronically worried people are more likely to lack confidence in their problem-solving ability, perceive anticipated problems as serious threats, become easily frustrated when dealing with a problem, and are pessimistic about the outcome of their problem-solving efforts. Complications occur when there seems to be no escape from a pending disaster, as in the diagnosis of a medical condition that forecasts an acute crisis or long-term disability.

The longer your time horizon is, the more there is to worry about. This is the way I feel about the extended future of my bipolar daughter and myself as I live alone through aging without resources sufficient to care for both of us. The recommended antidote for worry is to examine and challenge its validity, accept the future is indefinitely uncertain, to live mindfully in the moment here and now, and to place your trust in some Higher Power by faith. You might also imagine the worst that can happen and plan to accept it. First century Stoic philosopher Epictetus taught, "There is only one way to happiness and that is to cease worrying about things which are beyond the power of our will." This sounds like surrendering to the inevitable changes in aging. Jesus recognized the problem and instructed his disciples, "Can any of you by worrying add a single hour to your span of life? Since you cannot do this one thing, why worry about the rest? Your Father knows what you need and will provide (as He sees fit.) So, do not worry about tomorrow, for tomorrow will bring worries of its own. Today's trouble is enough for today" (Matt. 6:27–34, Luke 12:22–31, paraphrased). That sounds like mindful living to me.

Which brings up two limitations of DBT in emotions regulation, in my view. It does not adequately deal with the intensity of emotions, and it assumes grief merely is a form of sadness. I think grief is a separate emotion reaction to loss that requires its own response. It seems to be a process given to enable people to adapt to losses, be they a loved one, a valued thing or a lifestyle as we get older. According to the Holmes-Rahe Life Stress Inventory, death of a spouse is at the top of the scale rated at 100. Divorce is second, but it does not even come close at 73. When somebody enters your heart, they never really leave. Life goes on when you desperately want the world to stop and take notice. When you add up more cumulative losses over time—including loss of the lifestyle you expected before the crisis emerged—your overall health can be threatened unless they are recognized and effectively grieved.

Dr. Gary Harbaugh and I wrote *Recovery from Loss* (2001) to meet that need. It relates grieving to personality factors and walks the reader through five tasks: Acknowledge the loss, absorb the feelings, find substitutes, detach from the investment in the past, and reconstruct a different life in the "new normal." Easier said than done, and it takes as long as it takes. But grief is easier for some people if you have a plan to follow. There is a difference between normal and abnormal grief, as with every emotion. Grief can get complicated. When it becomes chronic and intense, grief can lead into depression if not treated. I know from experience. However, Jesus declared, "Blessed are those who mourn for they shall be comforted" (Matt. 5:4).

Grief also is an emotional response to loss of the lifestyle you expected, which no longer may be possible as you get older due to many changing circumstances. Plans don't always work out and things change. People die, and families get dispersed. As the late Beatle, John Lennon said, "Life is what happens as you are making other plans." When you realize this is the new normal, it can be very difficult to accommodate the necessary challenges, physical, spiritual, mental, and emotional. Shakespeare wrote this instruction in *The Tragedy of Macbeth*, "Give sorrow words, the grief that does not speak knits up the oer wrought heart and bids it break." You will need someone who is willing to listen without judging or trying to fix things that are broken which cannot be fixed. Grief needs to be expelled like a bad meal that upsets your stomach. When it is not expelled, it can result in constipated emotions, which can back up for years if they are not processed and released. If a loss is not processed at the time, a future loss may trigger old wounds that still need to be healed.

Support groups can provide a safe place where you can share emotions with others who have common concerns and help each other. Scripture says, "Carry each other's burdens, and in this way you will fulfill the law of Christ" (Gal. 6:2–4). There are support groups for people with just about every chronic illness, but you may need to search a bit to find them. They have their place, maybe in providing social connections, but they are not for everybody, especially introverts, as they can present more self-disclosure than you may find comfortable. Sometimes, undirected support groups concentrate on discussing problems with no solutions. Browse the Internet for help from official organizations dealing with your need. When your distress becomes urgent or critical, seek professional help. If trauma and shock after a critical loss is your concern, find a counselor who can help you work through the process of recovery from loss qualified to treat "trauma and stress-related disorders," a professional definition in the *Diagnostic and Statistical Manual.*

I found that emotions come in a wide range of intensity from mild to severe. From short term to long term. From acute to chronic. They can cross a boundary of intensity and time that shifts them into pathology. DBT deals primarily with the normal range of emotions. But sometimes, strong emotions get out of bounds and cause physical symptoms that may become critical, which is called a conversion reaction. The physical symptoms can create more emotions causing a closed loop of increasing disability until you reach a breakdown point; you feel overwhelmed, you cannot focus your thoughts on anything but the emotion, your mind shuts down and stops processing information. Your normal life feels damaged beyond repair and life takes on a surreal mood that destroys your serenity. It is difficult to define when this boundary is crossed, but you can tell it when you feel it. Like when anger becomes rage that turns into violence. Then, switch to the skills in distress tolerance in the next lesson. When any emotion interferes with life so much you become saturated with it and even disabled, it is passed time to see your doctor and get appropriate treatment. I entered therapy when my emotions transitioned to post trauma shock and depression. If you feel negative emotions are running out of control, please seek professional help.

As a defense mechanism while under emotional stress, some people may emotionally detach, which becomes a background for anxiety and other disorders if it sets you up for conflicts between self-care and needs of the others in the situation. Some experts in resilience suggest intentionally detaching from the situation—mentally, emotionally, and physically—if only temporarily to get some badly needed respite from incessant stress. It can be expressed as an "I don't care" attitude about the chaos in caregiving. I wrote the book titled *Creating Serenity in Chaos* to meet this need. Detaching comes in two forms: doing it consciously to gain some healing relief from stress, and what happens unconsciously as a defense mechanism to protect the mind from panic and permanent harm. It also can be a deliberate mental attitude, which avoids engaging the emotions of others to provide some distance by getting away from problems. This form of detachment does not necessarily mean withholding empathy; rather, it allows the sufferer to achieve the space needed to rationally choose whether or not to be overwhelmed or manipulated by disabling feelings. The person may be physically present but moves elsewhere in the mind and in a sense is not there, making them sometimes appear preoccupied.

Survivors with this need to detach from troubling situations often have emotional systems that are in overdrive. They may avoid activities, places, and people associated with any traumatic events they have experienced. They may disassociate from the here and now to avoid the pain that comes with the source of their discomfort. They may remove themselves physically from the situation and leave normal housekeeping and personal needs undone, at least for a short time. Others may do it mentally by thinking of other things, attending a movie, or reading a book. If they cannot see any way out, momentarily detaching and a little escapism can be okay as a defense mechanism. As with everything, detaching comes with benefits and burdens. It can reduce your distress, but also may leave your family with a feeling of loss and abandonment and leave you with a feeling of guilt. If it becomes chronic, detachment from reality is considered a result of anxiety disorder.

Anxiety may be an appropriate response to the fear of the future that comes when the threat is real. There are some good and sufficient reasons to be anxious when your personal future is being threatened. As such, the cause of anxiety should be confronted and treated properly. This can be done with cognitive therapy, prescription drugs and some types of supplements, notably Kava root, which has some research to support its usefulness. The recommended antidote is to engage life as much you can, absorb the emotions and let them emerge, rise, and leave because this, too, shall pass. Consult your doctor if momentary detachment has morphed into chronic anxiety (www.calmclinic.com).

The universe is composed of necessary opposites such as hope and despair, joy and suffering, independent and vulnerable, indispensable and insignificant called dialecticals. So, there are positive emotions, including love and joy, gratitude and serenity as well as negative emotions. You can learn to identify and to cultivate those to help balance the negativity of aging challenges, like giving up your driving privilege or moving to assisted living. Although it seems that negative emotions are unwelcome intruders, positive emotions may be both experienced and created from positive intentions. It isn't easy or quick, but with enough will power, it is possible to foster positive emotions by associating with positive people and attending events that provide positive emotions, even as your personal freedom must transition to surrender when the time comes. The benefits of more happiness and better health seem to be worth the burdens of making the effort. Here is a list of positive emotions compiled by psychologist, Barbara Fredrickson from her book, *Positivity* (2009). They can be a powerful resource in developing your personal resilience.

Joy. Think of the most positive and memorable experience you've had. A time when you felt safe, happy, and comfortable. This was probably a moment where you experienced joy. Joy comes from delightful and cherished experiences and raises our well-being where we feel light and vibrant.

Gratitude. This entails an emotion or attitude of appreciation where we acknowledge some benefit we have received. Gratitude can revolve around anything you feel great appreciation for and occurs during the times when you feel thankful for someone or something in your life. Apostle Paul instructed to "give thanks in all things for this is the will of God for you" (1 Thess. 5:18).

Serenity. This emotion comes along when things are going just right. You may experience a state of peacefulness and tranquility. Your mind isn't flooded with worries, and you're able to just sit back and relax. Serenity comes from those moments of stillness and calm where you can just be in the present moment.

Interest. Interest comes from being curious or engaged in something. It's a state of intrigue and wonder, where you want to know more and are pulled toward an object of interest. When feeling interested, you are open to new experiences and have a desire to explore the world around you.

Hope. This is a belief and feeling that things will turn out for the best. It's knowing our current problems aren't permanent and that the future is still promising despite tough circumstances. A hopeful person will believe that what they want will be obtained, and no matter how difficult the circumstances, they have faith that they will be able to do something about their situation.

Pride. This comes from feeling dignified and important in what we do or have accomplished. It's not about having an overwhelming sense of self-satisfaction but having accomplished something that is valued and feeling proud about this. It may come along from a sense of purpose and meaning in our accomplishments and offers an increase in confidence to expand the belief in our potential to do greater things.

Amusement. Whenever we experience fun, humorous, and playful situations with others, we are being amused. We can get amusement from laughing with others at a funny joke, watching a funny movie, or playing a fun game or activity. Amusement helps us build connections with others. (I really do have a sense of humor, but I have very little use for it in my situation.)

Inspiration. This emotion comes from experiencing a very moving and uplifting experience, such as those times when we see true goodness or where someone goes above and beyond the ordinary. Amazing feats of intellect, strength, and agility can lead to inspiration. A moment of inspiration draws us in and really stands out as an instant of excellence.

Awe. The notion of being awestruck comes from feeling wonder and reverence toward something extremely powerful and admired such as human compassion. This emotion may come from experiencing natural phenomena, such as the Grand Canyon, a beautiful sunset, or the crashing of ocean waves and the vastness of the universe. It can also come from amazing creations of art or highly impressive developments. Awe also can be a reaction to negative events such as hurricanes or tornadoes, flash floods, forest fires, and disease epidemics, wars, and crimes, etc. These are moments when we realize how insignificant we really are compared to the vastness of the world around us. Nevertheless, we must be indispensable as well as insignificant, or we would not be here, like a grain of sand on the beach or drop of water in the ocean. *This may be the emotion that drives me to conclude there is a power above all religions that explains such things, that is the God above gods.*

Love. Love is the compilation of all of the above emotions. Love is a feeling of strong affection and personal investment, where we have a very positive feeling of connection toward another person. This feeling may be enhanced from laughing and having fun together, or from kind and selflessness acts. Love is a combination of all the emotional states coming together throughout our lives. Jesus said there is no greater love than to give yourself for your friends, and to love your neighbor as yourself (Luke 19:27–37, John 15:13). This may be what he was referring to when he said, "Give and it will be returned unto you…with the measure you use it will be measured unto you" (Luke 6:38). In the King James Bible, love is translated as charity (1 Cor. 13:4–8). Science now is beginning to discover that unconditional charity is good for personal well-being. Giving as you are able helps you feel better.

Although it is an emotion discussed in DBT, for some reason, happiness is not on this list. Perhaps it is considered a thought more than an emotion. There are no objective tests to measure the presence of happiness, so it is mostly a self-reporting condition that is highly subjective. It can be defined in many ways, but people seem to know if they have it or not. Someone said to be happy, people need something to do, somebody to love, and something to look forward to. Unfortunately, it seems that our society is pushing old people further away from this ideal. Assisted living residences try to provide a safe housing arrangement with some amenities and relief from daily chores of housekeeping, but they are unavailable in many areas and too expensive for most of the baby boomers. So, as people age in place, with or without families, they gradually become socially isolated and disconnected from the community after they can no longer get out with other people. There does not seem to be enough public awareness or political will to change the situation any time soon.

Happiness has been discussed in philosophy since the ancient Greeks and now is a popular subject of research in psychology. The Greater Good Science Center in the University of California at Berkeley conducts a free online course called the Science of Happiness, which integrates many approaches to this elusive human desire. Happiness also is the objective of expert blogs at www.pursuit-of-happiness.org. Happiness seems to be as much a mental attitude as it is an emotion and means different things to different people. Happiness can be related to external circumstances and to internal response to aging situations. However, research seems to indicate that attempting to pursue happiness actually can make it more elusive. Learning about happiness is not the same as becoming happier.

People seem to have a life-long threshold for experiencing happiness driven by inherited DNA combined with their learned experience, which external events may not change very much. It seems to be a temporary response to achieving some goal, need, or want, which are replaced with new ones again and again as soon as they are fulfilled. No matter what happens, good or bad, we seem to return to the happiness set-point that each one is given. Abraham Lincoln observed that people are just about as happy as they make up their minds to be. He must have said that before the Civil War. Inventor of air conditioning, Willis Carrier, said the way to be happy is to imagine the worst that can happen and plan to accept it. First century Stoic philosopher Epictetus said, "No one is ever unhappy (or happy) because of someone else." You can decide if you agree with them or not. That may seem to be trite and dumb when you are contemplating chronic illness with no escape possible. Happiness seems to be something that both exists and can be created to some extent. It seems to be cultivated by compassion and loving-kindness to others in need through selfless service—what UC Berkeley psychologists call the greater good. They found that happiness is correlated with gratitude, health, contentment, compassion, and longevity, but correlations do not prove causation. Nevertheless, it would seem to be a beneficial aspect of aging, which you can add to this lesson on emotions regulation (www.greatergood.berkeley.edu).

Research in neurology reported by Dr. Robert Lustig, MD, is exposing a difference in the brain from experiencing pleasure and happiness. Pleasure can become addictive as it upsets the balance between brain neurotransmitters serotonin and dopamine. Dopamine is related to pleasure and fuels excitement. Serotonin is related to happiness and promotes calm. Pleasure is an immediate gratification that wants to be repeated, like using a cellphone for human connection instead of personal interactions. Facebook executives admit to making it addictive intentionally. Pleasure is about momentary getting from sensing effects—eating chocolate cake or smoking weed or sex. It turns out the more pleasure addiction you get, the unhappier you are. Happiness is more of a long-term condition than an effect. As such, it is more satisfying and rewarding if it is based more in giving than in getting. There are some food supplements marketed to increase serotonin, but they should be vetted thoroughly. Choose carefully and consult with your doctor about these alternatives. The advice from Dr. Andrew Weil, MD, may be helpful if you wish to explore a healthy lifestyle with him online (www.drweil.com), (*The Hacking of the American Mind*, 2017), (*The Chemistry of Calm*, 2011).

Hopefully, this discussion helps you consider the wide range of positive emotions that may help to balance the negative challenges for better resilience in aging. Dr. Fredrickson claims a large part of experiencing these positive emotions is choosing to do so. She has found it can take up to three positive emotions to offset one negative emotion. Begin making a choice to be open-minded and letting in moments of inspiration, joy, and interest, while working to cultivate hope for the future and gratitude for the present in your role as senior citizen. And go easy on yourself when you feel unhappy sometimes. Life is not all a bed of roses; it comes with thistles as well as blossoms—another example of the necessary opposites in the universe. Research indicates that it is healthy to make room for negative emotions plus positive emotions as they occur called emotional diversity.

Realize that all emotions are contagious, so practice "catching" positive emotions of your choosing and fighting off the negative ones. There are mirror neurons in the brain that mimic emotional situations in others, which helps explain the crowd enthusiasm at sporting games and the group sadness at funerals. So, go to places and hang out with people who can help you enjoy some positive emotions. Bottom line is, emotions—both negative and positive—are necessary and beneficial in their normal form. You cannot eliminate them from the experience in aging, but you can learn to employ their benefits without being overcome by their burdens. If you work on it, you may create more resilience and produce less chaos in the last quadrant of life. Like the kid found digging through a pile of manure in the barn said, "There must be a pony under here someplace." There is a lot to know about emotions that is beyond the scope of this book. You might do an Internet search to get more information. Browse "emotions" (www.goodtherapy.org).

Here is an assignment for homework. Notice an emotion, name it, and talk back to it. Say, "I am feeling an emotion right now. I think it is (x). I know it is normal and will pass if I do not encourage it to stay. So, I will be patient, absorb it while it lasts and let it go when it passes." Nothing comes to stay, and everything comes to pass. Keep a list of both negative and positive emotions as they happen during your family chores. Practice letting them happen and letting them go. Seek out some opportunities to experience positive emotions. Repeat often and add personal comments to your notebook. It is your personal diary of progress.

Distress Tolerance

First, notice this lesson is about tolerance of distress and not eliminating it or even reducing it. The goal of distress tolerance is to transform unbearable stress into normal human misery while making the best of what you cannot change without making things worse. Basically, stress is the reaction caused by any event or situation that causes you to feel removed from your comfort zone called homeostasis, physically, mentally, or emotionally. Much research indicates that some stress is needed to stimulate personal resilience so it must be necessary, or it would be eliminated by now through human evolution. Stress comes with life of the aging process, and men seem to be more vulnerable than women in general. The more that is learned about stress, the more complex biochemical reactions in the body appear to get. Stress can be a spur to action and self-improvement, but too much is too much when it becomes distress. Distress is defined as an aversive state in which a person is unable to completely adapt to stressors and their resulting stress and shows maladaptive behaviors as a result. It can be evident in the presence of various phenomena, such as inappropriate social interaction (e.g., aggression, passivity, or withdrawal) and the emotional crises of acute loss. Distress is the opposite of eustress, a positive stress that motivates people.

Eustress comes from the Greek root *eu*, which means "good" as in euphoria. Eustress is when a person perceives a stressor as positive. Distress stems from the Latin root *dis* as in dissonance or disagreement. It may be further defined as a reaction to the gap between what is and what you want; in other words, the failure of accommodating freedom and surrender—two sides of the same coin. It can include being stuck in traffic, having your day off ruined by rain, or losing money in the stock market, loss of a job, death of a loved one, divorce, or a serious illness. It also can include frustration with the lack of progress in recovery from loss or the futility of it. Some stress can be a beneficial motivator, but distress is a threat to the quality of life. It is when a demand of living vastly exceeds a person's coping resources. Stress can come from both physical and emotional challenges that tax our ability to cope, and the defensive reaction also can be physical or emotional. It can come from interactions among family members and medical providers in addition to social contacts. When it goes out of normal bounds, stress becomes distress.

Dialectical behavior therapy (DBT) defines distress as the tendency of some people to experience negative events as overwhelming and unbearable. When you realize the cause is life-threatening or the "new normal," it may invoke trauma and fear when it seems to take over your normal life. Not only must you rearrange your schedule, resources, and priorities, but you also must find the resiliency to handle emotional reactions. People with a low tolerance for distress can become dysfunctional at relatively mild levels of stress, and they may react with self-harmful behaviors or actions that create more stress. Stress reactions to a threat are regulated by a wide variety of brain regions, including the limbic system, prefrontal cortex, amygdala, hypothalamus, and stria terminalis. Through these mechanisms, stress can alter memory functions, immune function, metabolism and susceptibility to diseases. Over the long term, distress can lead to diminished mental health and/or increased risk of physical illness; to avoid this threat to your well-being, distress must be managed.

Maybe you're having that proverbial "bad day," or perhaps a rough few weeks: Feeling down, anxious, overstressed, as if you're one breath away from the "last straw." If so, you may be surprised to learn doctors say it is part of the human condition. The presence of anxiety, of a depressive mood, or of a conflict within the mind does not stamp any individual as having a psychological problem, because these qualities are indigenous to the human species. But if living on the "last straw" has become your way of life, experts say there's something on your mind that needs attention. The key is how often you are feeling this sense of distress, how bad it gets, and how long it lasts; that is what can help determine the seriousness of your situation.

To help you gain some important perspective on the stress in your life, experts helped WebMD put together this list of symptoms.

If many of these signs seem true for you, speak to your family doctor and request a complete physical. If everything checks out okay, ask your doctor if you might benefit from professional counseling.

Sleep disturbances. If you're sleeping more than usual or less than usual, if you can't fall asleep or wake up after only a few hours and can't go back to sleep, distress may be looming large in your life. If you have recurring disturbances of sleep more than once or twice a week, and there are no physical reasons your doctor can identify, your problem may be linked to a psychological problem—most commonly, anxiety or depression.

Dramatic weight fluctuations/changes in eating patterns. Have you gained or lost a significant amount of weight without any changes in your diet or exercise regime? Do you find yourself constantly thinking about food or feel repulsed by the thought of eating? If so, experts say it could be a sign of emotional distress. Constant preoccupation with food, weight, and body image is a sign that an eating disorder is sapping energy from other areas of life. In older women, loss of menstruation in conjunction with changes in appetite can also be a sign of trouble.

Unexplained physical symptoms. If, despite a complete physical exam and even a visit to a specialist or two, no one can find a reason behind your physical complaints, it may be your body's way of letting you know that your mind is in distress. Unusual symptoms that resist the medical workup can be a sign that your body is expressing some kind of upset. Problems commonly linked to distress can include headaches, difficulty breathing, a rumbling stomach, diarrhea, constipation, and chronic pain.

Difficulty managing anger or controlling your temper. Are you fine when you're by yourself but frequently get provoked to an explosion by your spouse, children, friends, or coworkers? If so, you may be on stress overload, a situation that is dangerous to your physical and mental health—and unhealthy for those around you. Not being able to control your anger is a sign of inability to manage stress. This is the one symptom that has the biggest impact on other people.

Some folks who have anger-management problems do not recognize the symptoms because they feel fine when they are by themselves. This is something that only comes into play in relation to another person—so it's easy to blame the other person for what is really your symptom. Even if you don't see the signs in yourself, consider counseling if your boss, coworkers, spouse, family, or friends are frequently telling you to calm down and watch your temper.

Compulsive/obsessive behaviors. Obsessions are repetitive thoughts which resemble worry and are accompanied by anxiety. Compulsions are behavioral acts designed to eliminate the obsessions. If your mind becomes so cluttered with obsessions and your day so filled with compulsions, life becomes completely taken over by anxiety and counterproductive rituals. Are you washing your hands—or feel a compulsion to do so—even though there's no logical reason? Are you constantly worrying that something bad is going to happen? Does it take longer to leave your home because you're bogged down with a series of "rituals," like touching things or rechecking locks, the stove, the computer? If so, you may have more anxiety in your life than you can handle alone.

Chronic fatigue, tiredness, and lack of energy. When the body cannot handle stress overload, it simply begins to shut down. And that is often manifested by a sense of extreme tiredness and fatigue. Feeling too "beat" to do the things you used to love—even when a physical checkup shows everything is all right—can be a sign of emotional distress and depression.

Memory problems. Lots of things can temporarily interfere with your memory, from the hormonal changes of menopause to a preoccupation with a work problem, to a lack of sleep and some medications. But it can also be caused by the stress of caregiving, a reaction to a traumatic event, or a chronic illness. If everything checks out okay after a physical, then anxiety, depression, or sometimes, an unrecognized reaction to a traumatic event you have yet to deal with may be behind your forgetfulness.

Shunning social activity. Did you love to go the movies with friends and now you don't? Do you seem fine at work but the minute you're home you jump into bed and just "veg out"? Are you turning down invitations because you simply feel better when you stay at home? Experts say all can be signs that your stress may be getting the best of you. Any significant change in social behavior for a long amount of time could indicate a stress overload. If phobias or fears of certain places or events are keeping you from doing what you like, then anxiety may be looming large in your life.

Sex is no longer fun. Are you going through the motions and not feeling the pleasure that sex once brought to your life? Do you love your partner, but just don't want to make out? If a physical checkup reveals everything is fine, then an underlying depression, or an anxiety disorder, may be behind your slump. Diminished sexual desire and inability to feel joy in sex can be a sign of distress. While that distress may be linked to your relationship with your partner, experts say just as often it could be linked to anxiety stemming from a chronic caregiving situation.

Mood swings and erratic behavior noticed by other people. While life may seem like business as usual to you, if friends or family members are commenting on your moody behavior, experts say pay attention. Listen to not only your own inner voice, but also listen to what you hear from your best friends, your neighbors, your spouse, your family. Others may have an observation of you that you cannot see. The greater number of people telling you that something is wrong, the more you need to pay attention (www.webmd.com).

Given that distress is so common among grieving people, what can we do about it? Realize that some stress is useful, and it must be necessary at this time in our evolution, or it would not exist. Stress can motivate people to do more and be better, as in studying for an exam or working harder to get a promotion—or being a better life partner. So, some stress is a good thing, but sometimes, too much is too much when it attacks your security and serenity. The antidote for distress is resilience, something you have and something you can develop, according to some experts. Resilience includes the ability to accept suffering as part of being human and to see a crisis as a challenge and not a disaster, with the outlook of a master while being a servant, i.e., the ability to adapt to change with empowerment, the reconciliation of freedom and surrender. Then we can turn to DBT for help.

There are four DBT distress tolerance skill categories: distracting, self-soothing, improving the moment, and focusing on the pros and cons. These skills are aimed at helping people cope with stress and absorb distress without avoiding it or making it worse. Dr. Linehan says if we try to avoid unavoidable distress, it not only intensifies but turns inward toward depression. I certainly can verify that.

Distracting: The first skill, distracting, helps people change their focus from upsetting thoughts and emotions to more enjoyable or neutral activities. This skill is taught with the acronym ACCEPTS.

A—is for *activities* and distracting oneself with healthy, enjoyable pursuits. Engage in activities that require thought and concentration. This could be a hobby, a project, work, or taking some classes in school.

C—is for *contributing* and doing things to help others, through volunteering or just a thoughtful gesture. Focus on someone or something other than yourself. You can volunteer, do a good deed, or do anything else that will contribute to a cause. Scripture says, "Carry each other's burdens, and in this way you will fulfill the law of Christ" (Gal. 6:2–4). My friend volunteers for working with NAMI, the National Alliance for Mental Illness. I collect clothing for homeless people.

C—is for *comparing* oneself to those less fortunate, finding reasons to be grateful while directing compassion to yourself. Look at your situation in comparison to something worse—like hurricane victims who lose their homes or disabled soldiers returning from combat, or aging relatives and neighbors worse off than you. Remember a time you were in more pain, or when someone else you know was going through something more difficult.

E—is for *emotion*, identifying the current negative emotion and acting in an opposite manner, such as dancing or singing when one is feeling sad. Do something that will create a competing emotion. Feeling sad? Watch a funny movie. Feeling nervous? Listen to soothing music. I like the "Easy Listening" channel on cable.

P—is for *pushing a*way, by mentally leaving the current situation and focusing on something pleasant and unconnected to the present circumstances. Defeat negative thoughts by pushing them out of your mind. Write your problem on a piece of paper, crumble it up, and throw it away. Put off thinking about the situation until a better time.

T—is for *thoughts*; diverting one's attention from the negative feelings with unrelated and neutral thoughts, such as counting items or doing a crossword puzzle or jigsaw puzzle or playing cards, or reading a book.

S—is for *sensations*, and distracting yourself with physical sensations using multiple senses, like holding an ice cube, drinking a hot beverage, or enjoying a warm foot soak. Pamper yourself a little bit, whatever you like, but don't overdo it with unhealthy behavior. Put a rubber band on your wrist and snap it to distract your attention when you feel distressed, and avoid harmful acts like cutting yourself or self-medicating with drugs, alcohol, and dangerous activities.

Self-Soothing: The second skill in distress tolerance is self-soothing by concentrating on using the five senses to nurture yourself in a variety of ways:

- Vision: Look at beautiful things such as flowers, art, a landscape, or an artistic performance.

- Hearing: Listen to music, lively or soft, or enjoy the sounds of nature such as birds chirping and waves crashing. Enjoy the voice of a relative or friend. I like to attend free concerts by the military bands in my area or dial up my favorite performers on YouTube.
- Smell: Use a favorite lotion or perfume or essential oil, light a scented candle, notice the scents of nature, or bake an aromatic recipe.
- Taste: Enjoy a healthy meal or indulge (rarely) in a decadent dessert. Experiment with a new flavor or texture and focus on the food's color.
- Touch: Pet an animal or give someone a hug. Have a massage, rub on lotion, or snuggle up in a soft blanket. Take a break from family caregiving to do something for yourself as simple as getting a hairdo or warm shower. If you can get a respite, take a short vacation, attend a movie, or walk in the park or go out to lunch. Sometimes, instead of doing something, it is helpful to just stand there doing nothing, letting yourself be human because where ever you go, you are there. There comes a time when just feeling what we feel is better than trying to fix something that cannot be fixed. However, if your feelings become disabling, seek professional help.

I like to think of flying above the weather where the air is calm and is untroubled. If you have ever flown above the clouds and looked down onto a storm from the top, you know what I mean. If you have not had that experience, try to find a picture of it or imagine it. I found such a picture of clouds from the top that I display as background on my computer. Another analogy would be slipping through the ocean depths in a submarine or scuba gear, far below the storms and turbulence on the surface. I often visit the public parks in my area, one of which dates to 1775. It gives me a different perspective on my own lifetime as I look over land walked by George Washington. In either image, the idea is to find a place that can improve your inner peace and serenity while showing compassion for yourself. A place where you can feel better inside no matter what happens outside if only in your imagination.

Improving the moment: In the third distress tolerance skill, the goal is to use positive mental imagery to improve your stressful situation. The acronym for this skill is IMPROVE.

I—is for *imagery*, such as visualizing a relaxing scene or visiting a soothing place. Let negative feelings melt away. This can be done closing your eyes and imagining some place in memory that you recall as serene and peaceful.

M—is for creating *meaning* or purpose from a difficult situation or from pain, i.e., finding the silver lining. Finding something to do for others in need will help.

P—is for *prayer*—to God or a higher power—for courage and surrender to be open in the moment, to accommodate freedom with surrender.

R—is for *relaxation*, by breathing deeply and progressively relaxing the large muscle groups. Listen to music, watch a funny television show, drink warm milk, or enjoy a neck or foot massage.

O—is for *one thing* in the moment, meaning the person strives to remain mindful and focus on a neutral activity in the present moment, living in the here and now.

V—is for vacation, as in taking a mental break from a challenging situation by doing something pleasant. This could be taking a day trip, attending a movie, or ignoring calls and emails for a few hours.

E—is for encouragement, by talking to yourself in a positive and supportive manner to help cope with a stressful situation. Find a confidant or counselor who listens with empathy.

Focusing on pros and cons: In this skill, the caregiver lists the pros and cons of tolerating the distress and of not absorbing the stress, that is coping through stress to avoid self-destructive behaviors. It can be helpful to remember the past consequences of not tolerating distress, and to imagine how it will feel to successfully tolerate the current distress and avoid negative behaviors. Through evaluating the short-term and long-term pros and cons, distressed people may focus on the benefits of tolerating pain and distress as stimulants to growth, and thereby reduce impulsive reactions.

If this sounds like a lot of work, it is. It may not be quick or easy, but research shows it is possible to feel better inside no matter what happens outside. It works if you work it. Besides, the pain of doing it is far less than the pain of not doing it.

Family members may experience many conflicting emotions when placed in the position of providing care for a grieving loved one. If you are caring for a family member, this applies to you also. Compassion, protectiveness, and caring may be intermingled with feelings of helplessness and being trapped, accompanied by self-guilt for not being able to fix the problem. Anger and depression may be included to make the situation feel unbearable. Someone said, "I really don't like the people I am supposed to love." Caregivers of chronic conditions in older loved ones are especially vulnerable, as in the worst of cases they may occasionally wish the distressed depressed person were gone. So, it is helpful if you practice the PEAA rule with your caregivers, providing praise, empathy, attention, and approval for what they do for you.

Patience also goes a long way. As Jesus said, what you give will be returned unto you, and with the measure you use, it will be measured to you (Luke 6:38). But when your freedom is jeopardized, the Christian response is surrender as scripture says:

> Bless those who curse you, pray for those who mistreat you. If someone slaps you on one cheek, turn to them the other also. If someone takes your coat, do not withhold your shirt from them. Give to everyone who asks you, and if anyone takes what belongs to you, do not demand it back. (Luke 6:28–30)

When the burdens feel overwhelming, self-destruction may seem like a reasonable choice, but it leaves more problems than it solves. These may leave survivors with feelings of guilt and remorse for being unable to prevent it. Living with the "if only" things you might have done differently may be disabling. If anything in the past could have been done differently, it would have. You can live with less stress if you believe nothing from atoms to galaxies can happen outside the will of God, and if anything in the past could have been different, it would have been.

It helps to tolerate distress if you take care what you think about. Researchers are learning that what we think about grows stronger and changes the brain, what they call neuroplasticity. Thoughts may not be facts, but they can drive your actions. Some experts claim if you think positively you get positive results, and if you think negatively, you get negative results. Research at the University of Wisconsin indicated people who think stress is killing them have increased chances of dying sooner than those who think stress indicates a challenge to overcome. Scripture says, "As a man thinks in his heart, so is he" (Prov. 23:7). Spending time absorbing emotional trauma, negative news, obituaries, and constant barrages of insulting comments is not healthy. This is not a new idea as first century Greek Stoic philosopher, Epictetus taught, "We are not disturbed by what happens to us, but by our thoughts about what happens to us. Events do not disturb men's minds, but their thinking does." Many centuries later, Shakespeare rephrased this thought in *Hamlet*: "There's nothing good or bad but thinking makes it so." It is all in your head, so they say. However, I have come to believe that we do not create our own thoughts. This assumption may explain why some people with serious disabilities seem to be happier than others who are better off. It also may explain those who commit suicide when they think they would be better off dead.

You cannot afford a single negative thought. That may be an exaggeration, but the fact remains that the way you think influences the way you feel and act in many circumstances. As my therapist would say, "Is thinking like that making you feel better or worse?" But positive thinking has its limits. Henry Ford said, "If you think you can or you think you cannot, you probably are right." Frankly, I don't think I will ever win a gold medal at the Olympics or be an airline pilot, or even a rich book author. And I am still working on positive thinking in what I judge to be negative situations. No one can convince me that watching the untimely death of my wife was a positive experience, and I find it impossible to think anything positive about its consequences, even as I accept it as God's will.

The term "positive psychology" was originally coined by the psychologist Abraham Maslow in the 1950s. The ancient benefits in positive thinking—some may call it positive spin—were applied to Christian faith through his innovative television ministry by the late Dr. Norman Vincent Peale and his book, *The Power of Positive Thinking* (1992, 2003). It has been sustained and expanded for secular use by Dr. Martin Seligman with his books and lectures through what he called "explanatory style." Dr. Seligman was contracted in 2009 to experiment with US Army soldiers to see if his ideas would help them to handle stress better. There are reported studies claiming that training in positive thinking can improve the resilience of disabled soldiers and their families. It has evolved into the Comprehensive Soldier and Family Fitness program in US Army Regulation 350–53 (*Learned Optimism*, 2006).

People with an optimistic explanatory style tend to give themselves credit when good things happen, but typically blame outside forces for bad outcomes. "The devil/serpent made me do it." They also tend to see negative events as temporary and atypical. On the other hand, people with a pessimistic explanatory style often blame themselves when bad things happen but fail to give themselves adequate credit for successful outcomes. British prime minister, Winston Churchill, said a pessimist sees the difficulty in every opportunity; an optimist sees the opportunity in every difficulty. On the other hand, someone said if you can keep your head while others are losing theirs, you don't understand the problem. My career was disrupted five times as I had to change jobs through no fault of my own. It was tough and became depressing, but I had a nonworking wife and two kids who depended on me whom I could not abandon so I dug in and kept moving.

Dr. Seligman says people with learned optimism assume they can surmount problems with self-confidence and appropriate self-talk responses to overcome adversity. However, Christians are advised to emulate Christ facing the inevitable cross, "May your will be done" (Matt. 26:42). "Whoever wants to be my disciple must deny themselves and take up their cross daily and follow me" (Luke 9:23). Some balance is needed in most crisis situations, that is reconciling freedom and surrender. The glass may be seen as half full or half empty, but sometimes, it is just too big. Dividing a major crisis into smaller segments might make them easier to manage than taking the whole situation in one gulp. Recall, inch by inch, life's a cinch; yard by yard, life is hard.

While positive thinking cannot remove all the problems grieving people face and would not be appropriate in all situations, it can help to reduce the stress of events you cannot control. After surviving Nazi concentration camps in WWII while losing his parents, brother, and pregnant wife, psychiatrist and founder of logotherapy Victor Frankl wrote, "Forces beyond your control can take away everything you possess except one thing, your freedom to choose how you will respond to the situation. When we are no longer able to change a situation, we are challenged to change ourselves." Unfortunately, we cannot seem to control ourselves as much as we may want to. He concluded, "What is to give light must endure burning" (*Man's Search for Meaning*, 1946). That is scant comfort for the survivors of all the families lost in the gas chambers, in my opinion.

Many people are asked to endure unthinkable suffering. Consider the homeless refugees who lost everything in the wars in the Middle East or vets returning from combat with lifelong disabilities or the destruction in Puerto Rico caused by Hurricane Maria. Positive thinking, mindful living, unconditional service, self-compassion, and gratitude seem to be essential ingredients for contentment, health and longevity. But it gets complicated. Either we have sovereign control over this response, or it comes from some Higher Power. Either God wishes to remove suffering and cannot, or he can but chooses not to, or he is the cause of suffering. Or, there is no God and stuff just happens, including what we think about it. What do you think?

First century Stoic, Epictetus taught, "He is a wise man who does not grieve for the things which he has lost but rejoices for those which he has." There is always something you can be thankful for I suppose, so focus on that even if it is moment by moment. I am thankful I can still trim my toenails, tie my shoelaces, and brush my teeth, and see the sky and smell the flowers, and hear good music and taste healthy food—and write this book, of course. I am thankful my health is as good as it is, and I do not have prostate cancer. Even thankfulness for apparent failure may be appropriate if we learn something from it. You might consider how Thomas Edison allegedly reacted to a thousand experiments that failed to disclose a material suitable for the filament in light bulbs, "I have not failed one thousand times because now I know one thousand things that do not work." You might say the same thing about finding the best medicine for your needs because it can require much patience and persistence through trial and error. I can look back on my life and see the growth that came with all that suffering. The scripture says, "Finally, brothers and sisters, whatever is true, whatever is noble, whatever is right, whatever is pure, whatever is lovely, whatever is admirable—if anything is excellent or praiseworthy—think about such things" (Phil. 4:8). The benefits of this ancient wisdom are being verified in modern psychology. The thing about wisdom is by the time we gain it there is little time left to use it. If that sounds depressing, let it stand.

Chronic stress is known to increase output of the hormone, cortisol that is secreted by the adrenal glands. This may cause a host of physical and mental symptoms which can reduce well-being and make distress tolerance more difficult to manage. Cortisol receptors are found in nearly every cell of the body which is why high cortisol affects so many systems. Chronically elevated cortisol from chronic stress puts you at risk for diabetes, osteoporosis, obesity, high blood pressure, heart disease, digestive disorders, infertility, chronic fatigue syndrome, thyroid disorders, immune system disorders, and, in rare cases, Cushing's syndrome. Elevated cortisol also contributes to brain fog, anxiety, depression, mood swings, memory loss, dementia, concentration problems, insomnia, and mental disorders of all kinds. Alarmingly, high levels of cortisol can kill brain cells by literally stimulating them to death. It also reduces the number of new brain cells being created by decreasing the production of a protein that stimulates new brain cell formation. High cortisol can energize the fight or flight response to danger that is outside the bounds of reasonable reactions to stress in aging. You might consider working on lowering your cortisol production if it is too high. This can be done with low glycemic foods, a healthy lifestyle, and related medications and supplements. For more information, do some research and ask your doctor for some advice. Perhaps, some testing would be helpful.

For homework, try something different. Go back over the DBT skills listed above and select some you feel comfortable with. Label and describe the stresses that are inhibiting your resilience and match up the skills to the distress. Begin to accept that resilience is not eliminating distress but rather learning how to carry it. Practice letting emotions flow through you instead of stifling them—in private if not appropriate in public. When you feel stressed, relax, focus on your breathing, close your eyes, and recite the mantra, "I am, here and now." Repeat and repeat and repeat some more.

(Caution: If you feel hopeless or trapped, or think you have no reason to live, get help immediately. Talking to a professional may help you make it through a crisis. Go to a hospital emergency room or a walk-in clinic at a psychiatric hospital or call your primary doctor. A doctor or mental health professional will talk to you, keep you safe, and help you get through this tough time. You also can call the National Suicide Prevention Lifeline at 1-800-273-8255. It's free and available twenty-four hours a day, seven days a week. It's confidential, so you can feel safe about sharing your concerns.)

Interpersonal Communications

Among all the things about human relations we take for granted is communications. The word covers such a wide range of information it is difficult to select what is most important for this book, so please forgive me if I do not cover topics of concern to you. My approach here is to discuss the subject from the viewpoint of interactions among committed couples and their immediate family members. Although it might not have made any difference, I wish I had learned these things before I got married. I did not learn them until after Rosalene was gone, but perhaps knowing them will help readers enjoy better relations from my experience.

Recall that we were separated the first year of our marriage, with me in Puerto Rico and Rosalene in college at Madison University in Harrisonburg, Virginia. There were no telephone connections or email, so I wrote long letters daily to her. Her responses were short notes accompanied by newspaper clippings, which I could not care less about. She opened the notes with "Dearest Hubby," and closed with "Love ye," but there was nothing much in between. I hungered for deeper vicarious intimacy with my absentee bride. This pattern set the stage for communications throughout the marriage. I talked so much she called me "motor mouth," and she said so little directly to me that I never really knew what she was thinking or feeling. The more important the issue was, the less she had to say about it. It was not until after her death that I learned what an "introverted feeler" was and how that aspect of personality impacts interpersonal communications. I only met three "extraverted feelers" and the contrast was stark. She also did not like to think about important issues and preferred to take things pretty much as they came. This also was part of the person who she was. Consequently, the burden of decision making fell to me about most things, and we led separate inner lives by not sharing our deepest thoughts with each other.

Thus, it is important to know something about personality factors applied to family communications. Without this understanding, people literally are mentally wired for conflicts. In my opinion, no couple should get married without a professional personality assessment and analysis. Every combination of personalities can be mutually rewarding if the partners understand and respect their different preferences of perceiving and judging the world. The details are beyond the scope of this book, but you can learn more online and from the books listed under "Communications" from the Center for Applications of Personality Type. (*The Type and Families Kit*, www.capt.org, www.16personalities.com) Refer to appendix A for a discussion of personality types in churches.

Here is how a widow explained her communication style using knowledge of personality type in caring for her dying husband—with permission. "I am an INTJ and my husband was an ENFP. As his disease progressed, I had to make an extra effort to express my feelings more openly and more often than I might normally have done, because I knew how important it was to him. Since sensing is my inferior function and there was a lot of practical stuff to deal with, I was aware that doing a lot of that was particularly draining, especially because I felt I didn't do it as well as some others might. On the other hand, I used my thinking strengths to plan and to research and collect information, to find out all I could about his disease, options for treatment, where to get help, etc. I had several people comment after he died that I seemed to handle everything so well. Of course, that was only true on the surface, but it did make me feel better since I felt so helpless about so many things." *To read an explanation of any two personality type combinations refer to "type2type" at* www.personalitypage.com.

I learned that not only do personality factors drive interpersonal communications, but cultural factors apply also. Rosalene was a preacher's daughter, and the preacher's family were not supposed to have any problems, at least none to be shared with the congregation. Therefore, she learned a "no-talk rule" when it came to dealing with concerns and problems of a personal nature. When it appeared that she was in distress by her body language and I probed for some discussion, she would say, "I don't want to talk about it." Rosalene suffered excessive bleeding during her periods, but she never openly disclosed her distress. So, I had to do a lot of mindreading, and, sometimes, I was wrong. Like the time I was leaving for work on Monday morning after a busy home chores weekend and as she kissed me good-bye, she said, "Boy, did you miss a hot weekend." How was I to know?

Then there is the matter of honesty. Perhaps it is better to leave some things unsaid if either partner cannot tolerate the truth or it would breach the relationship. It is difficult to anticipate the reaction you may get from some people who can harbor resentment without disclosing their true feelings. I learned that most people, if not all, want praise, empathy, attention, and approval (PEAA). Provide these and you make a friend. Do the opposites, and you create an enemy. Of course, this instruction applies to behavior that you want and should be withheld from behavior that you do not want. Everyone has an "inner critic" they learned from social experience. There may be aspects of ourselves we do not like. It bears watching your attitude about yourself and to avoid projecting what you don't like about yourself onto others you may love.

The key is making it about you instead of about them by using "I statements," which focuses attention on your personal needs and wants. An assertive I statement is nonjudgmental, expresses feelings and opinions, and reaffirms your personal rights. The best way to use this communication technique is by customizing the following sentence: "I feel [emotion], when you [the behavior], because [explanation]." Follow up with what you want with some benefit attached: "I would feel [emotion], or I would do [something] if you would please [desire]." Avoid personal attacks that begin with [You]. As in, "You make me sick." *Not*. Or, "It looks like you are gaining too much weight." *Not*. Compare with, "I really like the way you look in that dress, or suit." It takes practice, so find a friend and play "let's talk" with them. Even if you obtained verbal communications training in school, chances are good this practice would offer more benefits than burdens. You can change bad habits that stress your relationship, but first you must recognize and accept the need to work on changing them.

Which brings up the topic of words called vocabulary. Humans have developed sounds to convey thoughts, ideas, and emotions in several thousand different languages. These sounds are conveyed by voice and in some form of manual writing. You may have been taught the pronunciation and meanings of certain words in school, or not. The number of words varies with nationalities, and usually, they are defined in dictionaries. The largest number of words, more than one million, seems to be in the Korean language. The *Merriam-Webster* third edition dictionary of English lists about 470,00 words. Most people know fewer than twenty thousand words, and some can get by with far less. New words are being created all the time, as the way computer jargon went from "program" to "application" to "app." Words are combined into sentences that come with certain rules of grammar. There are nouns, pronouns, adjectives, verbs, adverbs, etc. The ways in which these elements can fit together are almost infinite and depend somewhat on the level and quality of education that one achieves. Two people who have different levels and quality of education likely will need to work on making themselves understood by an intimate partner.

The most important aspect of words is their meaning. The meaning of words is subject to cultural standards that vary with time, and there are "good" words and "bad" words. There are words that uplift people and words that tear them down. There are words of social acceptance and words socially unacceptable. The meaning of words that control communications is that in the mind of the recipient and not the transmitter. So, it is important to have a mutual understanding of the words flowing back and forth if effective communications are to be achieved. The social impact of words is especially important to politicians, those of "many tongues." There are so many ways to say the wrong thing in the wrong place at the wrong time that public speaking is fraught with potential for harm. Abraham Lincoln reportedly said, "It is better to keep quiet and to be thought a fool than to speak up and remove all doubt." Thus, it is important to assess the way your words are interpreted and to make amends when the situation calls for redress of grievances. That is, if you want to sustain the relationship.

So, maybe that will encourage you to get on with this lesson. In dialectical behavior therapy (DBT), interpersonal effectiveness refers to the skills, which help us to attend to relationships, balance priorities versus demands, balance the "wants" and "shoulds," while building a sense of mastery and self-respect. In order to increase your effectiveness in dealing with other people, you need to clarify what you want from the interaction, be as specific about that as you can, and identify what you need to do and are willing to trade in order to get the results you want. In a word, negotiate.

Like most of the instructions in DBT, the communications work also uses the model of acronyms to present the principles as follows:

DEARMAN—helping us gain our objective:

> Describe the current situation,
> Express your feelings and opinions,
> Assert yourself by asking for what you want, or by saying no when necessary,
> Reward the person—let them know what they will get out of it. Be
> Mindful of objectives without distraction (broken record technique, ignoring attacks).
> Appear effective and competent (role play, use your acting skills).
> Negotiate alternative solutions—I would…if you would…

The relationship, how important is this relationship for me? What do I want this person to feel about me after this interaction? What do I need to do in order to keep this relationship? Are the burdens worth the benefits?

Keeping the relationship, GIVE—Use a:

> *G*entle manner without attack or threat, express
> *I*nterest in the other person,
> *V*alidate the other person without judging, use an
> *E*asy manner (with a little humor?) Remember that everyone needs/wants praise, empathy, attention and approval (PEAA).

Self-respect. What do I want to feel about myself after this interaction? What do I have to do to feel that way about myself?

Keep your self-respect. FAST—be *fair* to yourself and others, make no apologies for being alive, *stick* to your values (not do anything I'll regret later), be *truthful* without excuses or exaggeration.

With effective communications skills, you also can avoid getting what you do not want. It is called boundary management. The description in their book titled *Boundaries* (2017) by Cloud and Townsend says:

> If you've ever wondered: Can I set limits and still be a loving person? How do I answer someone who wants my time, love, energy, or money? Why do I feel guilty when I consider setting boundaries? Unpacking the ten laws of boundaries, Drs. Henry Cloud and John Townsend give you biblically based answers to these and other tough questions, and show you how to set healthy boundaries with your spouse, children, friends, coworkers, and even with yourself. You'll discover firsthand how to reclaim your freedom to walk as the loving, giving, fulfilled individual God created you to be.

It may be worth a read, if you remember it is bible based. However, it is a good idea to respect the boundaries of others also. Every legal adult has a right to the privacy of their person, their space, and their possessions, and especially to the privacy of their thoughts. You could remember to ask for permission before you invade their legal boundaries, even those of your spouse.

Boundaries may involve things like housekeeping, money, food, time, activities, sex, etc. Whatever is important to you, set your limits and stick to them. Boundary limits can be conditional or unconditional. Conditional limits can be negotiated, unconditional limits are deal breakers. After my wife died, I was a very needy man. One of my suppliers was a younger woman who told me, "Lew, don't be hitting on me because if you do, you will lose a friend as well as a supplier." I got the message, and we are still friends to this day. Conditional limits leave the door open for possible future changes. "I can't right now, but if [...] then it may be possible." I get that response sometimes when I ask a widow neighbor to lunch. If you accompany unconditional limits with any threats, be able and willing to enforce them—without exception. You don't have to make any excuses or explanations…just a "no thank you" or "I have other plans," will do. But make a benefits and burdens analysis first before you accept or reject any invitation. (Refer to appendix B)

However, this process works the other way too, as when your request of someone might be rejected by them. It is important not to take it personally and to give the other person the same freedom and control that you want. Remember, communications is a two-way process and do unto others as they want you to do unto them—unless the burdens are not worth the benefits. A wise man once said, we have one mouth and two ears, so use the latter twice as much as you use the former. When you are listening, listen and do not interrupt as that could indicate you are more interested in transmitting than receiving. And remember that the meaning of what you say is in the mind of the receiver, so ask for confirmation to round out the loop.

I must admit I am not very good at this. I do not like conflicts, and I hate negotiating. There, I said it. My INTJ personality makes it difficult to own and to display my introverted feelings. And the ENFP personality of my wife also gave her the same introverted feelings too.

Consequently, throughout our marriage a lot of things never got discussed, and when she needed my care it got even worse. She shut down discussion of emotional issues merely by saying, "It upsets me." I sincerely regret all the unfinished business. Later, I did some behavioral research and after much study, I decided my favorite personality in a partner should be INFJ because of their extraverted feelings. Unfortunately, I only found two of them and neither one worked out, but for other reasons. In fact, the communications between us was much better. So, what I am saying is to take it easy and slow if you find this lesson to be troublesome. Like the late opera diva Beverly Sills said, "There are no shortcuts to anything worthwhile." Developing skills in interpersonal resilience would be in that category.

One more thing about interpersonal relations deserves repeating because I need to read it again myself. Regardless of their age or condition, everyone wants praise, empathy, attention, and approval (PEAA). This is powerful medicine, and a little of it goes a long way. The human ego loves it. In his practical book, *How to Win Friends and Influence People*, (1930) Dale Carnegie emphasized that most people are more interested in their own lives than they are in yours. In short, everyone wants to feel important and special. So, ask open-ended questions and be responsive with attention, praise, and approval. The late poet, Maya Angelou, said, "People may not remember what you say, but they will remember how you made them feel." Practice the modified golden rule: "Treat others as they want to be treated." And if you don't know, ask. If two people want the best for each other, they both win. Just remember that, and your interpersonal communications will go much better. I promise.

Maybe you detected this lesson is about maintaining some self-control in the challenges of intimate relationships. The desire for control is the basic problem in human affairs, and loss of it can be a most troubling aspect of marriage, often leading to divorces. In his poem *Invictus*, William Ernest Henley wrote some words of comfort. When you feel soul sick from the incessant chronic challenges in communications, these words may provide some resilience: "I am the master of my fate, I am the captain of my soul." Or, you can believe that God controls everything from atoms to galaxies in the universe, and all is happening as it should, or it would be different. Whichever you believe, I think it must be God's will.

PART IV

Resurrection from Hell

As I stated elsewhere, the founder of dialectical behavior therapy, Dr. Marsh Linehan, observed that troubled people must go through misery to get out of hell. After the loss of my beloved spouse untimely at age fifty-two, I can say that she was putting it mildly. I could not find words strong enough to express what was happening to me. All the plans, all the assumptions about life, and how things should be were shattered beyond repair. I came to realize that some things that are broken cannot be fixed. This is why we have cemeteries and junkyards. I feared for my survival and fell into deep depression several times. At those times, I would spend the whole weekend in bed with the covers pulled over my head to avoid seeing the light. When I went to the office, I just sat there staring at the walls for hours. It is a wonder they did not fire me. When in such unspeakable distress, it may be possible for some survivors to find comfort and solace in their faith among supportive friends. I had neither. The church members all ran away, and the friends were all hers and not mine. My coworkers realized I was in crisis, but all they could do was stand by and watch it unfold. I searched for some source of relief, and slowly, I began to see light at the end of the tunnel. When I could, I read dozens of books and eventually saw a pathway that took me far beyond our family traditions into a world of new possibilities. Being a writer, I began journaling my discoveries, which I describe here in a brief form. To get the full story, you would have to read all my books, so this summary will have to suffice for this one. Visit: www.betterlivingbetterdyng.com.

Growing Beyond the Bible

As noted above, I was a committed Christian, a deacon, and a Sunday school teacher during my marriage to Rosalene. But when I went to the pastor for grief counseling and he said he could not help me, my faith in the traditional belief of my family was no longer helpful or comforting. Not only did I become a skeptic, I became a contrarian, which I discussed in my book titled, *The Bible You Don't Get in Church*. So, now I must go beyond the story of my life, grief, and losses to discuss growing beyond the Bible. The Bible has served a basic need of humans to believe in something that is transformative. It provides solace facing the indefinite uncertainty about a future that is unpredictable. However, the basic problem I see with Christianity is that very few people can imagine and accept that God causes destruction of his/its own creation because they are taught all human behavior and suffering are caused by their inherited will to sin. But scripture does not support this one-sided use of proof texting or cherry picking. If the Bible is the Word of God, it should not be censored at will in my opinion.

The Bible was composed by various writers over a period of 1,500 or more years. Some of its stories chronicle events that are simply fantastic. Perhaps it is as C. G. Jung said, "All the works of man come from their active imagination." Albert Einstein said imagination is more important than knowledge, and Napoleon said imagination rules the world. Nothing can be done that is not first imagined, from going to the moon to planning dinner. Imagination enables humans to remain connected with others in their absence and thus to provide social cohesion among members of tribes at a distance. We are perhaps the only species on earth that can imagine the future and make plans for it, including the afterlife. Many people cannot seem to accept the notion of nonexistence after death, so they invented stories to imagine life after life. Unfortunately, imagination cannot distinguish between the real and unreal so the mind can easily be deceived, as with actors, politicians, magicians, and preachers. Perhaps the best example is the imagined friendship Christians have with a resurrected savior as the hymn states: "What a friend we have in Jesus, all our sins and griefs to bear." Except when he doesn't. Poet, Robert Frost said, "It is hard to get into this world and hard to get out and what lies in between makes no sense." He also wrote, "Lord, please forgive my many little jokes on thee, and I will forgive thy great big one on me." He lost his wife and five of six children by his age of sixty-two and lived until age eighty-nine to think about it. The only way I can make sense of life is to imagine a God above Gods, i.e., generator, operator, destroyer, who controls everything from atoms to galaxies, including all the world's many religions.

The Bible says, "You saw me before I was born and scheduled each day of my life before I began to breathe. Every day was recorded in your book!" (Ps. 139:16). It is God who directs the lives of his creatures; everyone's life is in his power (Job 12:10). That assumption seems to negate free will before we are born. We may not be able to see God, but we can see his creation, and a lot of it stinks pretty badly. Consider all the dangers including tornadoes, hurricanes, earthquakes, floods, fires, diseases, crimes, poverty, etc. God creates laws and causes people to break them, so he can save some at his own discretion. He seems to be indifferent to the consequences of his creation even when they cause suffering. "I, the Lord, do all these things" (Isa. 45:7). Nothing is impossible with God no matter how random or improbable or destructive events may seem. Somebody always wins the lotteries in life, good people suffer, and bad people prosper. Even the so-called "accidents" seem to be inevitable when you consider all the causes that go into causing them as links in an unbreakable chain all the way back to the First Cause. Causal determinism proposes that there is an unbroken chain of prior occurrences stretching back to the origin of the universe and before that.

All correlations are not causes, but experiments in quantum mechanics disclosed that changes in subatomic particles affect others even at some distance apart. It appears that causation does not always depend upon correlations. If any event in the chain were different, the outcome would be different. As such, even a flat tire is an act of God when you think about it. The tire depends on discovery and processing and marketing of rubber, which comes from the rubber tree, and the nail depends on the discovery and processing of iron into steel when it is merged with other metals, which are natural elements of the earth, and they both must arrive the same place at the same time. The probability of all this being a random occurrence is beyond imagination. Dr. Marsha Linehan, originator of dialectical behavior therapy, thought about it and concluded everything that happens is inevitable.

When he was asked why he writes horror novels, Stephen King replied, "Why do you assume I have a choice? I cannot imagine doing anything else." Whatever happens seems to be the inevitable culmination of untold events one linked upon another. Current events are links in a chain leading into the inevitable future called causal determination. And all the links are caused by God. So, what appears to be free will may be an illusion, necessary as it may be to justify punishing people who break the laws. There are no speed limits in Montana, so there are no arrests for speeding. The Bible says, "Sin is not charged against anyone's account where there is no law" (Rom. 5:13). But there is a catch. St. Clement wrote, "God rules with two hands, Christ in one and Satan in the other." If we are created in the "image and likeness of God" as the Bible says, then are we not all composed of both a Jesus and a devil? And the one that wins is the one he chooses. Recall, Jesus performed exorcisms on people who were involuntarily demon possessed, and he healed a man blinded since birth to show his power, all in the will of God of course. In scripture, as in life, there does not seem to be any one-sided coins.

The God that creates the beauty in nature and the infinite cosmos also creates the carnivores who kill and eat each other for food and the cosmic black holes that consume entire galaxies, plus the saints and criminals. God creates drugs for medicine and drugs for addictions, and he makes people susceptible to both. God creates peacemakers and warmongers, diseases and cures. In modern terms, cybersecurity experts who created benefits of the Internet and the World Wide Web are balanced with cybersecurity criminals who use it for nefarious purposes. Recall the Bible says, "I make peace and create evil/calamity. I, the Lord, do all these things" (Isa. 45:7). Can you believe that?

Swiss psychiatrist, C. G. Jung, said, "Man's suffering does not derive from his sins but from the maker of his imperfections, the paradoxical God." Here, we have an explanation of why Adam and Eve got off on the wrong foot. God made them do it. They did not disobey intentionally. God put the serpent up to tempting them and made them susceptible to temptation. Jesus petitioned in the *The Lord's Prayer,* "Lead us not into temptation" (Matt. 6:13). If God does not tempt people, why bother asking him not to? Perhaps Jesus recalled his temptations by Satan during his sojourn in the wilderness that initiated his ministry, all in God's will, of course. You know, the One who in the beginning created the heavens and the earth and everything in it (Gen. 1:1). And who created humankind with the will to disobedience, as any parent with a two-year-old child or rebellious teenagers will attest.

Unfortunately, most people cannot believe that free will is a necessary illusion. We have no free will, so we must believe in free will, and that must be God's will. Scientist, Albert Einstein, said man can will what he wants, but he cannot will what he wills. Nothing, from atoms to galaxies, happens outside the will of God, including what we believe. Everyone must necessarily be where they are doing what they are doing instant by instant, or they would be someplace else doing something different. If you can believe that, this work may be very important to your spiritual growth even if you are disabled, live in poverty or a prison, or are driven from your home in a war. With this belief system, you can feel good inside no matter what happens outside, if you work it. If it does not help you feel better inside, perhaps it will help explain why you feel so badly on the outside. If you still believe the Bible is the Word of God, that must be God's will because it makes no sense otherwise. And, of course, you can reject this whole thing and just go outside and play.

Most people adopt the religion they are taught in childhood. Rarely, does anyone consider the origin of their belief and research other options. Some people are Mormons, some are Muslims, some are Buddhists, and some are Christians—plus hundreds more religions that are scattered around the world, even among indigenous tribes who never heard of the Bible. God makes atheists and agnostics also. C. G. Jung said, "The shoe that fits one pinches another," including all those sitting in churches, synagogues, and mosques, each of whom get something different from the service. Human perception of the benefits in any practice of religion has been studied extensively for centuries with no generally accepted conclusions.

Studies show that the practice of any religion can have positive, neutral, and negative effects in the lives, health, and stress of the faithful. Prayer—personal, intercessory, and distant—produces a wide range of results in various situations. The idea that your brain can convince your body a fake treatment is the real thing—the so-called placebo effect—and thus stimulate healing has been around for centuries. Tests of new drugs usually compare results with a benign substance assumed to have no effect and, often, the drug produces little more benefit than the placebo but with significant negative side effects. Faith and belief sometimes seem to cause temporary physical results, but the mechanism between mind and body still has not been established, even in hypnotism such as that practiced by some faith healers. Sick people may feel better temporarily after prayer, but they still die.

Moreover, some people change their minds with new information, and some don't. Some people reach a plateau in life and stay there, and some continue growing until they die. The late world-famous cellist, Pablo Casals, continued to practice several hours each day into his eighties because he said, "I think I am still making progress." All in God's will, of course, as there can be no other. That may sound too simplistic, but it is the only plausible answer after you strip away all the futile attempts to find a better explanation for what happens in the world. In fact, it is the ultimate answer to the ubiquitous "why" question—God's will—because that reply includes everything in the universe from atoms to galaxies.

The church of my wife and the tradition of my family could not contain the growth that comes with openness to all the religions of the world. I had to develop a belief system that accommodated the world as it is. I learned there is no benefit in judging anyone who follows a different pathway, and no one can take the walk for another. C. G. Jung said, "Your pathway is not my pathway. Therefore, I cannot teach you. The pathway is within." Like the lyrics of the late Frank Sinatra proclaim, we all do it our way because that is the only way we can. If it is all God's will, then you can feel good inside no matter what happens outside, because Jesus said, "The spirit gives life, the flesh counts for nothing. The words I have given you are full of spirit (a.k.a. energy) and of life" (John 6:63). He also said before you criticize the speck of sawdust in the eye of another to remove the plank in your own vision (Matt. 7:3).

Faith and reason seem to be mutually exclusive sides of human nature, and faith trumps reason in the religious experience. It must if people are to believe that God sent his only son into the world to save the people he created from their sins, which he gave them the freedom to accept or reject. Since it makes no sense otherwise, there must be some force or power superior to reason behind the common human desire for religious experience. American theologian, William James, described religious experience thus: "No adequate report of its contents can be given in words. Its quality must be directly experienced. It cannot be imparted or transferred to others. They are more like states of feeling than like states of intellect. No one can make clear to another who has never had such a feeling, in what the quality or worth of it consists, and something in you absolutely knows the result must be truer than any logic-chopping rationalistic talk, however clever, that may contradict it. They are states of insight into depths of truth unplumbed by the discursive intellect. They are illuminations, revelations, full of significance and importance, all inarticulate though they remain; and as a rule, they carry with them a curious sense of authority for after-time" (*The Variety of Religious Experience*, 1902, 2016). However, there is more to life than religion, unless we live in a monastery.

The secular and nonsecular aspects of life seem to be mutually exclusive. Most people spend a few hours per week in church while the rest is spent in earning and living while wearing a theatrical mask or artificial persona. It seems to be taboo to discuss work and homelife at church and to discuss religion in the workplace in our culture. Jesus instructed, "Enter through the narrow gate. For wide is the gate and broad is the road that leads to destruction, and many enter through it. But small is the gate and narrow the road that leads to life, and only a few find it (Matt. 7:13–14). This seems to narrow the Christian life so much there is little chance of achieving it unless you live in a monastery. However, Apostle Paul said the new Christians should continue in the secular life they had when called, earning their living by honest work. "The one who is unwilling to work shall not eat" (2 Thess. 3:10). There were no professional clergy in the incipient church, and Paul apparently made his living as a tent maker.

But Paul changed quickly.

> Don't we have the right to food and drink? Don't we have the right to take a believing wife along with us, as do the other apostles and the Lord's brothers and Cephas? Or is it only I and Barnabas who lack the right to not work for a living? If we have sown spiritual seed among you, is it too much if we reap a material harvest from you? (1 Cor. 9)

By the end of the first century, the Church had become formally organized with a hierarchy of deacons, bishops, and even a pope. Thus, professional Christians, like the Jewish temple priests, began to live a life separated from the real world of the working classes like the rest of us. They constructed a religious environment that keeps the secular and nonsecular in separate compartments. If there is to be a bridge between the secular and nonsecular experiences of life, we must search beyond the Bible to construct it. For a complete discussion of conflicts in the Bible, read my book, *The Bible You Don't Get in Church*.

Among the many words of William Shakespeare often quoted are these from *Hamlet,* Act 1, Scene 3 where Polonius says: "This above all: to thine own self be true. And it must follow, as the night the day. Thou canst not then be false to any (one)." Socrates reportedly said at his trial, "The unexamined life is not worth living." C. G. Jung said those who look outward dream, but those who look inward awake. Jung called this personal inventory the process of individuation and said it is the primary task in the second half of life. He also said it is difficult and costly.

Jungian analyst, Dr. James Hollis, expanded this theme in his book, *Creating a Life: Finding Your Individual Path*, 2001. This book, among his other books, is his interpretation of Jung's concept of personal individuation. This relates to the rigorous midlife transformation of those conscious enough to be interested in plotting a course to spiritual and psychological wholeness. Dr. Hollis reinforces the promise of both what is attainable and what is at risk if one embarks on the quest by stepping out of our comfortable box into the unknown. Here are some edited comments from reviewers of his books.

By the first years in school, children are socialized into conformity, leaving little opportunity or acceptance for the continued development of their infantile spontaneous personalities. In our youth, we construct a personality for the ego to defend itself against the scary realities of life. Throughout life, we mistakenly identify with our provisional personality, which adapted to deal with family and cultural social situations in our life experience. We submerge the wholeness of self and authenticity we were born with which is driven down into the subconscious mind. The defenses for our wounds (not the wounds) are the principle causes of conflicts in our relationships with ourselves and others. In our culture, people are valued more for what they do than for who they are. Many people are so busy human doings they never really learn how to be human beings, much less achieve their full potential. If they did, the world would be a drastically different place. The late anthropologist, Margaret Mead, said, "Never doubt that a few dedicated people can change the world. Indeed, that is the only thing that ever has."

The second half of life can bring the realization that the old beliefs don't work very well. But most of us continue banging our heads against the rock of the old ways hoping for a new result. What is unconscious in our lives will either be projected onto others, either in terms of criticisms against the other or in admiration of role models, or it will manifest in our life as our destiny. The second half of life offers the challenge to replace mindless reactions with conscious reflection. It challenges us to dig deeply to know ourselves so we can develop our own unique individuation. One is challenged to fill in the chinks left by the first half of life, the transition from the life of ambition and accomplishments, however grand or small they might be, by listening to and obeying the promptings of the soul/psyche. This confrontation between the inner and outer has been called a midlife crisis. It raises the existential questions of why we are here and where we are going—man's search for meaning. Some people say it is better to struggle at something you love than to thrive at something you hate. Think about it.

In his own Socratic fashion, Dr. Hollis poses many excellent questions without presupposing the answers. He tells us that the passage through life will be successful only after going through our suffering and finding out from where it originates, burying our old set of values and ways of being, and giving birth to others that are more in tune with our soul's desire. Perhaps this transformation was foreseen by Apostle Paul in his description of Christians. "The old has gone and the new is here" (1 Cor. 5:17). Hollis makes a virtual map for this journey into our subconscious storehouse, but we must each live out the questions for ourselves. Instead of the pursuit of happiness, Hollis recommends the persistent search for meaning in life. The greatest mystery remains where we came from and where we are going (www.amazon.com).

The walk of life to self-realization, what C. G. Jung called individuation, may be out of reach for most people, and the journey is a lonely walk. Jung said, "Your pathway is not my pathway. Therefore, I cannot teach you. The pathway is within." However, whether we make this journey or keep playing the games is not ours to choose because I think the pathways we are given are not our own conscious creation. Read on. There is a light at the end of this tunnel.

My New Revelation

The untimely death of my wife at her age of fifty-two thrust me into a deep grief that I never anticipated. Dr. Marsha Linehan, founder of dialectical behavior therapy, said we must go through misery to get out of hell. I felt like I was in hell on earth. If that were to be my future, I did not want to live any longer in that condition. I had to find an answer to the ubiquitous question, "Why?" My knowledge of the Bible and my roles as a deacon and Sunday school teacher were no comfort. I feared for my survival, and I hated God for the willy-nilly habit of killing his creation with wars, diseases, so-called natural disasters, carnivorous predators, crimes, all in the process of pruning his creation as spoken by Jesus (John 15:2). If you doubt the ability of humans to create havoc for themselves, watch a mixed martial arts match, male and female. I had the most difficulty with this scripture: "Endure hardship as discipline; God is treating you as his children. For what children are not disciplined by their father?" (Heb. 12:7). That seemed to me like a poor rationale to help incipient Christian churches accept the brutal domination of Rome.

Swiss psychiatrist, C. G. Jung, said his suffering mental patients got sick because they lost whatever was provided by their religion, and they were not cured until they got it back. He said the treatment required making peace with God, but I just could not do it after my wife died. I needed a different view of God. Leon Trotsky (1879–1940) observed, "Life is not an easy matter. You cannot live through it without falling into frustration and cynicism unless you have before you a great idea which raises you above all kinds of perfidy and baseness." The Bible no longer provided such a great idea for me.

So, I began a deep search for a new spiritual belief that would accommodate the world as it is. After two decades of research into many beliefs, meditation, and therapy, I found my solution, or rather it found me. I call it belief in theofatalism (a.k.a. theological determinism.) This belief came to me through discovery of the Hindu worship of the Trimurti composed of three Gods—Brahma, Shiva, and Vishnu; the gods of creation, maintenance, and destruction. They appeared to me as a unitary trinity of Generator, Operator, Destroyer—that is God, not to be confused with God in the Bible.

This trinity seems to be a more practical and realistic depiction of reality than the inferred trinity in the Bible. This is not a threefold God that looks and acts like people he created in his own image. I see it as the prime force in the universe that controls everything from atoms to galaxies—Generator, Operator, Destroyer—as three in one. This is the God above gods in all the man-made religions that creates those religions as was proposed by the late theologian, Paul Tillich. Nothing seems to happen outside the will of this God, including the scriptures about God in the Bible and worship of the gods in all the other religions of the world. This belief also would have to include the arguments for and against belief in theofatalism. With this belief, you may be able to feel good inside no matter what happens outside. Perhaps like Job, who lost his wealth, family, and his health, we could say, "The Lord gives and takes away, praise to the Lord" (Job 1:21).

Unfortunately, our society values happiness and success as essential goals and focuses on the material world while devaluing the immaterial spiritual world. Moreover, Christians claim that God does not cause suffering, which originated in the original sin of mankind (Zeph. 1:17, Rom. 3:23). Things do not work out as planned, people disappoint, and all beginnings come with endings. The good suffer and the bad prosper. Perhaps we are given problems to learn how to solve problems. There are only three options: (1) God wants to prevent suffering, but he cannot; (2) God could prevent suffering, but he chooses not to; or (3) God causes suffering. Theofatalism concludes that the latter is the most logical option based on the evidence. This belief likely is troublesome for many Christians to consider, much less accept. It is difficult to worship a God that is the light at the end of the tunnel. It was difficult for me to accept, too. If you fit into this group, please reserve your judgment until you finish reading this discussion.

The evidence for theofatalism is too extensive for this brief discussion, but it will suffice to provide sufficient grist for the argument. I found many resources in fields of science, sociology, anthropology, psychology, philosophy, religion, politics, and economics leading to the inevitable inference of a God above all gods, as was proposed by the late theologian, Paul Tillich. Just as science assumes the existence of undetectable black holes and dark matter in the cosmos by inference from the laws of gravity, so can theofatalism be inferred from logical reasoning. Albert Einstein said, "Human beings, vegetables, or cosmic dust, we all dance to a mysterious tune intoned in the distance by an invisible player." Shakespeare wrote that all the world's a stage and men and women merely are the players, each with their entries and exits. C. G. Jung wrote, "God is the name by which I designate all things which cross my path violently and recklessly, all things which upset my subjective views, plans and intentions, and change the course of my life for better or for worse." The Reverend Paul Tillich (1886–1965) wrote, "Faith consists in being vitally concerned with that ultimate reality to which I give the symbolical name of God." Christians who cherry pick scriptures claim that God gave man freedom to accept or reject his only son as savior. But Jesus said, "No one can come unto me unless the Father causes/enables them" (John 6:44, 65). "You should say if it is the Lord's will we will live and do this or that" (James 4:13–16). I bet you don't get that in church.

Christians often say, "God is in control," without thinking much about what that really means. British theologian emeritus, Paul Helm, says, "Not only every atom and molecule but also every thought and intention are under the control of God." If we can assume that all thoughts and behaviors come from God, including thoughts about God, then a lot of the suffering and insanity—maybe all of it—in the world begins to make sense. For example, Pentagon reports said the US Army launched missiles from drones that mistakenly killed more than 7,500 civilians to kill about 340 ISIS fighters in Syria, called collateral damage. And people living in the most impoverished parts of the world continually make babies who are doomed to starvation. All in God's will, of course. This view of God as Generator, Operator, Destroyer permits all the pieces of the puzzle of life on earth in its many forms—plant, animal, and human—to fit together. With belief in theofatalism, you can avoid all remorse and guilt, praise and blame for events in the past you wish were different because if they could have been different, they would have been.

The Bible affirms this belief in scriptures you are not likely to get in church as follows: "The Lord kills and makes alive; The Lord makes poor and makes rich; He brings some low and lifts some up" (1 Sam. 2:6–7). "I make peace and create evil/calamity" (Isa. 45:7). In this context, the Hebrew word for "evil" is translated elsewhere in the Bible as spoiled, bad, adversity, trouble, sinful, misfortune, calamity, so take your pick. "When a disaster comes to a city, has not the Lord caused it?" (Amos 3:6). "Though you build your nest as high as the eagle's, from there I will bring you down, declares the Lord" (Jer. 49:16, Obad. 1:4). "Who has spoken and it came to pass, unless the Lord has commanded it? Is it not from the mouth of the most high God that good and bad come?" (Lam. 3:37–38). "When times are good, be happy; but when times are bad, consider this: God has made the one as well as the other" (Eccles. 7:14). Those readers who may correctly say these scriptures are legacy Old Testament references, consider this from the New Testament: "[God] is over all and through all and in all" (Eph. 4:6) and "from [God] and through him and to him are all things" (Rom. 11:36). The Quran says this to Muslims; "No calamity comes, no affliction occurs, except by the decision and preordainment of Allah" (S:64.11). What God creates, it also destroys.

If you believe the Bible is the infallible Word of God, it follows that the only reasonable answer to the ubiquitous question—why?—is it must be God's will, or it would be different. This assumption would include beliefs of atheists and agnostics, as well as the religious, because GOD—generator, operator, destroyer—makes them all. After all, the man-made holy books, including the Bible, are found to be impotent and flawed. This belief can provide some firm ground on which to stand. Theofatalism has all the generation, operation, and destruction—everything that happens in the universe—covered, from atoms to galaxies, in my opinion.

Theofatalism comes with five principles: (1) everything must be necessary or it would be different, including all the many different belief systems; (2) people make decisions subconsciously they do not control while assuming the expected benefits are more valuable than the burdens, including their beliefs in unprovable religions; (3) the universe is composed of necessary opposites, as in the ancient Chinese symbols of yin and yang, which includes the good and evil in each person; (4) the future is indefinitely uncertain, including what happens after death, and (5) GOD—Generator, Operator, Destroyer—is everywhere in everything from atoms to galaxies as immaculate immanence.

It follows from the above principles of theofatalism that to be content, which is the Buddhist solution to suffering, one must follow five steps in ADTDA thinking:

1. *Accept* what is moment by moment because it must be necessary or it would be different.
2. *Detach* from what you cannot change and wish was different because it hurts too much not to.
3. *Transcend* the need for control because in reality you don't have any as the brain has a mind of its own.
4. *Don't fight* with God, because you cannot win. You must walk the labyrinth pathway you are given.
5. *Assume* there are no mistakes, only predestined choices and inevitable consequences.

All in God's will, of course.

Theofatalism accommodates both acceptance and rejection of this reasoning as well as adoption of other belief systems. Everything must have its complementary opposite because God never made any one-sided coins, such as up and down, in and out, sweet and sour, good and evil, male and female, anima and animus, cold and hot, pessimism and optimism, active and passive, content and discontent, creation and destruction, predator and prey, criminal and victim, love and hate, joy and suffering, sickness and health, rich and poor, pain and pleasure, positive and negative, light and dark, truth and falsity, first and last, win and lose, war and peace, birth and death, maze and labyrinth, random and destined, insignificant and indispensable, heaven and hell, Christ and Satan. Knowledge and wisdom also have their opposites. King Solomon wrote that much wisdom brings much sorrow and much knowledge brings much grief (Eccles. 1:18). Anything apart from its opposite is meaningless, like one hand clapping. The opposites are required to make the whole. F. Scott Fitzgerald said, "It is a mark of maturity to hold the opposites and still function normally."

Psychiatrist, C. G. Jung, said there is the thing/idea and the symbol of the thing. The Reverend Paul Tillich (1886–1965) wrote, "Man's ultimate concern must be expressed symbolically, because symbolic language alone is able to express the ultimate." The symbol in Catholic churches is the crucifix and in protestant churches it is the empty cross. The symbol of theofatalism depicted on the cover of this book is the ancient labyrinth inlaid in the cathedral of Chartres, France (1200 CE) where there is only one pathway for each one to follow. Unlike the dead ends and random pathways of a maze, which are intentionally designed to confuse and to frustrate, the labyrinth has no barriers, and it definitely is not a random walk.

After we emerge from the center at birth, we go out into the world following the pathway we are given through stages of infancy, childhood, youth, and adulthood. After we pass midlife, we go back again through stages of maturity, seniority, contemplation, and mortality to the origin of life. C. G. Jung said the challenge in the second half of life is to recover the authentic spontaneous personality we were born with that got submerged by the social influences of our culture—what he called individuation. Happiness may be found in recovering the self we are born with before we die. Few people ever make this journey much less reach the destination. I think the spirit/

energy occupies the body during our transient walk of life and leaves at death. The body returns to basic elements of the earth, but the energy of life can neither be created or destroyed. The labyrinth symbolizes this pathway through life.

The Reverend Lauren Artress wrote:

> Walking the labyrinth has reemerged today as a metaphor for the spiritual journey and a powerful tool for transformation. This walking meditation is an archetype, a mystical ritual found in many religious traditions. It quiets the mind and opens the soul. Each step unites faith and action as travelers take one step at a time, living each moment in trust and willingness to follow the course set before them. (*Walking a Labyrinth,* 2011)

Theofatalism says there are many different pathways in life, one for each of us, and we cannot fail to take it. Labyrinths in several sizes are available for sale. I keep one at my dining table and finger walk through it after each meal. Visit www.bwatsonstudios.com. For more discussion, refer to my book titled, *A Labyrinth Walk of Life*.

Buddhist nun, Pema Chodran wrote, "The spiritual journey involves going beyond hope and fear, stepping into unknown territory, continually moving forward. The most important aspect of being on the spiritual pathway may be to just keep on moving" (*When Things Fall Apart,* 2016). And it all must be God's will, or it would be different. The Bible says, "It is God who directs the lives of his creatures; everyone's life is in his power" (Job 12:10, GNT). It seems like this applied to Jesus also when he prayed, "My Father, if it is possible, may this cup be taken from me. Yet not as I will, but as you will" (Matt. 26:39). If you need more scriptures consider this:

> Go to now, you that say, today or tomorrow we will go into such a city, and continue there a year, and buy and sell, and make money: Whereas

> you know not what shall be on the morrow. For what is your life? It is even a vapor, which appears for a little time, and then vanishes away. Therefore, you ought to say, if the Lord wills, we shall live and do this or that. (James 4:13–15)

If it is true, this belief must apply to everyone, everywhere, all the time, including those who believe in free will and those who don't. Gravity does not ask for your permission, and neither does God. This is the God beyond gods described by Paul Tillich.

Perhaps this belief in theofatalism will be confirmed at some future time, or maybe not. Every great new idea that challenges establishments must survive attacks and rejection before it is accepted. The existence of atoms was just a theory until they became visible through a miraculous electron microscope. The law of gravity was not confirmed until nearly eighty years after it was proposed by Sir Isaac Newton. Classical artist, Vincent van Gogh, committed suicide when he could not sell his paintings, but now they sell for millions of dollars. Although it is impeccably logical, theofatalism may need to run the gauntlet of trial before it is acknowledged.

Critics of theofatalism may pose two arguments. One lies in its apparent negation of conscious free will, which people seem to need to believe. They say if we have no free will, then hope for improving our lives disappears under a blanket of depression and despair. How come some people yield to temptation while others do not, if not from free will? Without assumed free will, all actions would be robotic, and people could not be held responsible for the results of their uncontrollable impulses. Assumption of free will is the international basis for jurisprudence because without it there would be no justification for laws or their enforcement. Apostle Paul wrote:

> Let everyone be subject to the governing authorities, for there is no authority except that which God has established. Consequently, whoever rebels against the authority is rebelling against what God has instituted, and those who

do so will bring judgment on themselves. (Rom. 13:1–7)

This scripture seems to express his condescension to the rule of Rome while Paul was a prisoner shortly before his final demise. It also seems to condemn all forms of insurrection and revolution, like the American Revolution and the US Civil War.

If Ralph Waldo Emerson was correct, and we all have within us the capacity for every crime, what separates the criminal from the saint? How come history repeats over and over as grand orators lead gullible followers into the abysmal pit? Examples include the Nazi regime of Germany under the endless propaganda of Adolph Hitler and may be with the "winning" harangues of President Donald J. Trump. He declared that he could walk down Fifth Avenue and shoot somebody without losing his base of supporters. Hitler wrote in *Mein Kampf* (1925) that it is not the best equipped or trained army that wins, but the most disciplined. If Hitler had become an architect as he wanted to, world history would be different. But his destiny intervened, and fifty-five million people died in WWII. He wrote, "The Jews knew that by an able and persistent use of propaganda heaven itself can be presented to the people as if it were hell and, vice versa, the most miserable kind of life can be presented as if it were paradise. If you tell a big enough lie and tell it frequently enough, it will be believed."

Jesus referred to his disciples as "sheep" (Matt. 15:24, Mark 6:34, John 10:2–7, 14–16, 21:17, 26–27). And he said if the blind leads the blind, they both fall into a pit (Matt. 15:13). All leaders are made by willing followers. That seems to be the best way to explain all the insanity and suffering in the world caused by leaders who attract many followers/sheep.

Proponents of free will also may argue that scripture claims free will is a gift from God as it lets people love and obey him because they choose to do so (Matt. 22:37, John 3:16, 14:15). But the Jews rejected him. "Jerusalem, Jerusalem, you who kill the prophets and stone those sent to you, how often I have longed to gather your children together, as a hen gathers her chicks under her wings, and you were not willing" (Matt. 23:37). However, free will is negated in other scriptures because there must be necessary opposites. Jesus said no one comes to him unless the Father calls/enables them (John 6:44, 65). The Jews who rejected Jesus did so because that was their destiny (Isa. 6:9–10, Matt. 10:13–15, Mark 4:10–12, 1 Pet. 2:8). Apostle Paul wrote that about everyone: "God has bound/consigned/imprisoned everyone over to disobedience so that he may have mercy on them all" (Rom. 11:32).

> For those God foreknew he also predestined to be conformed to the image of his Son, that he might be the firstborn among many brothers and sisters. And those he predestined, he also called; those he called, he also justified; those he justified, he also glorified. (Rom. 8:29–32)

This claim is repeated throughout the New Testament. As noted above, Paul also lamented his inability to control his sinful behavior near the end of his life (Rom. 7:18–19, 24). Note also that Paul was called to his ministry; he did not volunteer for it. Neither did any of the twelve apostles. "You did not choose me, I chose you" (John 15:16, 19). King David proclaimed his life was predestined. "You saw me before I was born and scheduled each day of my life before I began to breathe" (Ps. 139:16). If people are born sinners destined for hell without a redeeming savior, where is the free will? Could belief in free will be a God-given illusion?

To the question of whether the Bible teaches determinism or free will, the answer is yes. You can find scriptures claiming both in the Word of God if you look for them. Hence, the principle of necessary opposites in theofatalism. And which you believe is God's will or it would be different.

Another criticism of theofatalism involves possibly confusing correlation with causation. Critics of theofatalism may claim that because two events are related does not prove they are causative. The theory of causal determinism says all events are inevitable because they are caused by previous events in a chain linking back to the First

Cause (a.k.a. causal determinism). Drug addicts exist because God created the plants that produce drugs and the people with ability to be addicted and then brought the two together. A flat tire happened because rubber was discovered in a rubber tree and processed into tires, and nails come from iron that is mixed with tin to make steel that is used to make nails, and they arrived at the same place at the same time. Our thoughts also are less free than we think. Baruch Spinoza (1632–1677) wrote, "In the mind there is no absolute or free will; the mind is determined to wish this or that by a cause, which has also been determined by another cause, and this last by another cause, and so on to infinity." Events occurring now are links in the chain of unknowable events in the inevitable future. By applying this idea to Rosalene, I can conclude our marriage and her illness and death were inevitable consequences of predestined events back to the beginning of human creation. All in God's will, of course.

Common sense would say people can do things differently than they do, but no one—neither saint nor sinner—can go back in time to do anything differently. I believe if anything in the past should have been different, it would have been. There is no place in theofatalism for remorse and regrets because it says there are no mistakes, only predestined choices and inevitable consequences. Humans are very adaptable as indicated by those who cannot live without their cell phones and autos and those who live in primitive tribes as hunter-gatherers. People have learned to live on earth from deserts to rain forests, from the arctic to the tropics and on isolated islands, in mansions with servants and in shacks without running water.

Here is the thing. Everyone evidently is where they must be, doing what they must be doing, including those living in mansions, prisons, hospitals, and refugee camps. If not, they would be someplace else doing something different. All burdens come with benefits, and the worst of circumstances present opportunities for growth even if we cannot help ourselves. Someone said if you cannot be near the ones you love, then love the ones you are near. Suffering souls stimulate compassion and charity among observers, and dare I say markets for caregivers. Even animals in distress can evoke emotional responses from human caregivers. Whatever your calling is, you don't have to search for your purpose, status, or place in life because you cannot avoid it. This idea is difficult to apply to refugee camps and prisons, but they must be necessary to fulfill the principle of necessary opposites.

Theofatalism acknowledges the opposing views of free will and causal determinism as necessary opposites in the same way that God is perceived in the Bible both as love and a raging fire (1 John 4:8, Heb. 10:27). God never made any one-sided coins. Theofatalism postulates that whatever people believe or eventually discover is the consequence of the will of God. Whether you agree or disagree also must be the will of God. Mystical writer Abd-ru-shin (a.k.a. Oskar Bernhardt), who was big on free will, intuition, and personal volition declared in *The Grail Message* (1941). "All teachings were at one time willed by God, precisely adapted to the individual peoples and countries, and formed in complete accord with their actual spiritual maturity and receptivity." Various people are Catholics, Protestants, Buddhists, Hindus, atheists, republicans, and democrats. God makes them all. Thus, belief in theofatalism removes intolerance from all beliefs.

Religions of some kind all seem to be necessary at this stage of human evolution. When we realize how insignificant each individual is in the scale of the space/time universe, many people seem to need belief in some Higher Power to offset their fear of annihilation. The hope of immortality seems to be a universal desire among homo sapiens. It may feel comforting to have a source to rely upon when needing help that is unavailable from people, even if it is imaginary. Without such a reliable source, people are more likely to seek a substitute in various addictions and unhealthy behaviors, membership in criminal gangs and loyalty to charismatic leaders. Of course, the necessary opposite view was expressed in his poem, *Invictus* (1888) by William Ernest Henley; "I am the captain of my fate, I am the master of my soul." Whichever view you take must be God's will, or it would be different, in my opinion.

The great mysteries of the world may or may not ever be resolved. The lot of mankind may not be to achieve a goal of any kind but rather to grow through struggles and problems that energize our souls. Without them, we would be stagnant piles of refuse fit only for the dung heap. I like the idea voiced by President Theodore Roosevelt in a speech he gave in 1910.

> It is not the critic who counts; not the man who points out how the strong man stumbles, or where the doer of deeds could have done them better. The credit belongs to the man who is actually in the arena, whose face is marred by dust and sweat and blood; who strives valiantly; who errs, who comes short again and again, because there is no effort without error and shortcoming; but who does actually strive to do the deeds; who knows great enthusiasms, the great devotions; who spends himself in a worthy cause; who at the best knows in the end the triumph of high achievement, and who at the worst, if he fails, at least fails while daring greatly, so that his place shall never be with those cold and timid souls who neither know victory nor defeat.

But don't beat yourself up if you seem to fall short of this ideal person. Albert Einstein said, "Man can will what he wants, but he cannot will what he wills. The answer comes to you and you don't know how or why." So, if you agree or disagree with this conclusion, never fear, because I believe that God is creating your thoughts as well as your actions. I conclude that nothing happens outside the will of God, including the acceptance and rejection of theofatalism.

Difficult and emotional as it is to accept our mortality, there are certain secular things that need attention before it is too late to help with the planning. They include such things as making a will or setting up a trust for your heirs, choosing the kinds of medical treatment you want or don't want with your primary doctor, filing a medical directive with your primary doctor, appointing a health care proxy and durable power of attorney, making advanced funeral arrangements, and discussing the way to spend the final good-bye time. This is called the conversation project by a group of the American Academy of Family Physicians (www.theconversationproject.org).

These arrangements can be complicated as laws vary from state to state, so it is best to engage competent legal aid. If you don't do these things, a court may have to appoint a legal guardian or conservator to manage your affairs when you no longer can. Check with your local office of Area Agency on Aging for help with the location and selection of advisors. You can find them by browsing the National Association of Area Agencies on Aging. Visit online at www.n4a.org.

Hospice advocate, Dr. Ira Byock, MD, recommends the four elements of a family terminal conversation to be: "I forgive you, please forgive me, thanks for everything, I love you, good-bye" (*The Four Things That Matter Most*, 2014). It is better to have this conversation while you are healthy than to wait until a medical emergency may make it difficult or impossible.

The most difficult of all issues may be deciding how much control you want over your personal death. You might die suddenly by stroke, heart attack, accident, or crime—or maybe not. If you have a choice, this decision will affect your survivors for the rest of their lives, so it deserves your serious attention. You can refuse treatment and stop eating and drinking—and die in two weeks. The options include dying at home with nursing support possibly under hospice rules, dying in hospital or nursing home among strangers possibly alone in your bed, or engaging your doctor to aid in your passing, which is legal in California, Oregon, Montana, Colorado, Vermont, and the District of Columbia. The Final Exit Network works on behalf of people and their doctors who want ultimate control over dying when they decide it is their time to go. For more information, visit www.finalexitnetwork.org. If you do not complete such plans, you may end up as Jesus warned his disciple: "When you were young you dressed yourself and went wherever you pleased, but when you are old someone else will dress you and take you where you do not want to go" (John 21:18). All in God's will, of course.

I don't know if I will ever see Rosalene again or not. Jesus said there will be neither marriage or giving in marriage in heaven because we will all be like angels (Matt. 22:30, Mark 12:25, Luke 20:35). I believe that, from atoms to galaxies, everything that happened in the past, everything that is happening now, and everything that will happen in the future must all be necessary, or it would be different. And that is enough. I close with this bit of wisdom from the great philosopher, Forrest Gump: "Life is like a box of choc'lates. You never know what you're gonna get." This is true here and in the hereafter. Living with the uncertainty in life may be the greatest challenge in being human.

If my story and discovery of theofatalism are helpful to you, perhaps you could organize a study group to help apply the benefits to other people who may need support in walking the pathway of life they are given. We must go through misery to get out of hell, and it helps if we have some company.

EPILOGUE

I got more comfort often from singing the traditional hymns in church than listening to the sermons. I will close with the lyrics to one of my favorites. A song which encourages us to lay up treasures not on earth but in heaven is "This World Is Not My Home." The text and music appear to have come from the southern African American spiritual tradition, but the author is unknown. Sometimes, they are attributed to Albert Edward Brumley (1905–1977). Brumley made what is undoubtedly the most popular arrangement of the song for his 1937 book *Radio Favorites*, and it is the one used in the vast majority of hymn books. My favorite performance of it was by the late Jim Reeves (Wikipedia).

This World Is Not My Home

This world is not my home I'm just a passing through
My treasures are laid up somewhere beyond the blue
The angels beckon me from heaven's open door
And I can't feel at home in this world anymore

Oh lord you know I have no friend like you
If heaven's not my home then lord what will I do
The angels beckon me from heaven's open door
And I can't feel at home in this world anymore

I have a loving mother just over in gloryland
And I don't expect to stop until I touch her hand
She's waiting now for me in heaven's open door
And I can't feel at home in this world anymore

LEWIS TAGLIAFERRE

Just over in glory land we'll live eternally
The saints on every hand are shouting victory
Their songs of sweetest praise
Drift back from heaven's shore
And I can't feel at home in this world anymore

APPENDIX A
A Christian View of the MBTI

The Myers-Briggs Type Indicator (MBTI) is a popular personality inventory that was first published in 1943. It is based on a theory of psychological types published by Swiss psychiatrist, Carl G. Jung in 1923. The MBTI was developed by Isabel Briggs Myers and her mother, Katharine Briggs, as a way to help people understand themselves and each other better. The MBTI was officially recognized and published by Consulting Psychologists Press, Inc. (CPP) in 1975. Studies seem to indicate that personality has genetic origins independent of home and social influence. Parents, homes, schools, churches, neighborhoods, and all the other environmental factors individuals experience when growing up appear to account for about half of adult personality preference as measured by objective self-report instruments such as the MBTI.

Many people have heard of the terms extravert and introvert and have unofficially tested their personalities or self-identified with a specific personality type using available online sources. Descriptions include general personality traits, strengths and weaknesses, best jobs for each type, best learning environments for each type, and even best romantic combinations of each type. The secular considerations of the MBTI notwithstanding, is the idea that there are different personality types biblical? Are personality types something Christians should consider? Are they helpful in any way in church fellowship?

The MBTI self-reports preferences in four different functions each of which can be either introverted or extraverted. These variations specify sixteen personality types. The functions include: (1) a focus on the exterior world (extroversion, E) or the interior world (introversion, I); (2) a focus on basic information (sensing, S) or interpreting and adding meaning to information (intuition, I); (3)

making decisions by first looking at logic (thinking, *T*) or by first considering the people involved (feeling, *F*), and; (4) a desire for things to be decided (judging, *J*) or being open to other options (perceiving, *P*). The sixteen personality types are identified as combinations of those four preferences. For example, *ISTJ* describes personality type that is basically introverted, focused on basic information, logical, and most comfortable when decision-making has been resolved. (*My preferred type is INTJ and that of Rosalene was ENFP. A lot of thoughts go through my head that never come out my mouth.*)

Possibly the most confusing aspect of the MBTI model is understanding the difference between thinking and feeling in the process of decision making and judging. Thinking depends upon and requires logical reasoning in reaching useful conclusions. Feeling is driven by emotions that are triggered by primitive aspects of the brain. Dialectical behavior therapy (DBT) includes discussion of the following emotions: anger, disgust, envy, fear, happiness, jealousy, love, sadness, shame, and guilt. Emotions are useful in life threatening situations and when time is of the essence. Mislabeling thinking and feeling is very common. People often say, "I feel that…" when they really should say, "I think that…" People can feel hot or cold, which are sensations, and they can feel happy or sad, which are emotions. But, they cannot feel that they are stupid or that someone hates them. Those are thoughts. Feelings and thoughts can be combined. For example, "I feel happy because I think Jesus loves me." Or: "I think my partner is cheating, which makes me feel angry." Feelings and thoughts both can be valid and invalid. In cognitive behavior therapy (CBT), one is taught to identify and label thoughts and emotions, to assess their validity, and to control the behaviors that ensue to make better decisions and judgments. Without these skills, relationships can be stressed and broken when actions are based upon invalid thinking and feeling.

The Myers & Briggs Foundation is careful to point out that no one personality type is better than any other personality type. Also, personality types are not indicative of ability or character. The types are simply offered as helpful tools in better understanding oneself. Personality type might be helpful in making choices, but it should not be the only tool a person uses to determine career path, romantic partners, or the like.

We know that all humans are made in the image of God (Gen. 1:27). We know that we are uniquely formed and that God fully knows us and fully loves us (Ps. 139). Nothing in the MBTI contradicts this. Simple observation tells us that some people seem energized by spending time with others (extraverts) whereas other people recharge best alone (introverts). The late theologian, Paul Tillich, described in *The Eternal Now,* 1963, a difference between loneliness and solitude that bears contemplating. "Language has created the word 'loneliness' to express the pain of being alone. And it has created the word 'solitude' to express the glory of being alone." The Bible leaves room for there being different types of people as well as for commonalities among the different types. It does not contradict biblical truth to classify certain general similarities among people.

The benefit of the MBTI for Christians is in helping us better understand ourselves to better serve God. Often, our personality traits coincide with God's call on our lives. For example, we might tend more toward introversion and have as part of our call being a writer. Or perhaps we tend more toward extroversion and find that God has asked us to host large-group Bible studies. Knowing our "natural" strengths can help us be attuned to the places where we can serve most effectively; knowing our "natural" weaknesses might help us avoid paths that would more easily trip us up.

Understanding personality types can also help Christians better love and serve others who appear to be different. For example, when we know that one of our friends tends more toward introversion, we'll know that time spent together one-on-one is probably more meaningful than time spent together in larger social settings. If our friend tends more toward extroversion, we'll know that he enjoys being included in social activities so we can be sure to invite him or encourage him to lead a study group. Understanding personality types also can help us more easily accept others. For instance, when an introverted friend says no to our invitation to a get-together, we might not take it personally. Or, when a person who is a "thinker" talks about the bottom-line in a church budgeting decision, while a "feeler" focuses on ways the money can be used to help people, we can recognize these are the ways God has naturally created them. Committees can make better decisions with contributions from several viewpoints.

One danger of the MBTI for Christians, or for anyone, is in making personality type inflexible and using it to justify stagnation. One's personality type does not excuse one's bad behavior, nor does it limit one's ability to change or to do and enjoy things not stereotypically within the type. An introvert is still called to share the gospel. An extrovert is still called to spend time alone with God. A thinker should still consider the people his decisions affect. A feeler is still expected to be a good steward. When God calls us outside of our comfort zone, personality type is not a reason to disobey. If anything, a call of God that challenges our natural inclinations gives us more opportunity to trust him and a deeper understanding that it is only his work in us that causes amazing things to be accomplished (Zech. 4:6). As Apostle Paul explained, the church is like a body with many parts, none of which are more important than others, and each part is equally needed for the benefit of all (1 Cor. 12:12–27).

I like to think of the four functions, sensing, thinking, feeling, and intuition as related to the physical, intellectual, emotional and spiritual aspects of being human. If they are understood in this light, becoming the whole person we can be involves moving up from data to information to knowledge and finally to wisdom in each of these four quadrants. The main problem here is, as was discovered by King Solomon, with much knowledge comes much sorrow and with much wisdom comes much grief. (Ecclesiastes 1:18) And by the time we gain wisdom there is very little time left to apply it. Perhaps that is how it is meant to be. For more discussion, read my book titled, *Better Living, Better Dying*.

The Myers-Briggs Type Indicator (MBTI) can be a helpful tool in understanding God's unique design of humanity and of yourself specifically. It hints at both the order and diversity with which God created the world, demonstrating his logic and his artistry. Understanding ourselves can help us better steward the gifts God has given us. Rather than try to become someone else, we can thank

God for his unique design and make the best use of the gifts God has given us. However, to get valid results, you must be truthful in answering the self-reporting questions. If you do, you may be pleasantly surprised (www.mbtionline.com, www.16personalities.com, www.personalitypage.com).

(Excerpted and edited from *Christian Counseling* (2006) by Gary Collins)

APPENDIX B
Making Better Decisions

Acceptance of the Bible and Jesus as Messiah/Savior requires a decision of most importance because your decision could determine where you spend eternity, if there is one. Decision processes could be a separate study. It gets complicated. Some modern experiments in neurology seem to show the brain makes decisions before we are conscious of them, but if that applies to all decisions is unknown. For example, consider how the brain controls breathing to balance excess carbon dioxide with oxygen intake. Much of our lives is conducted unconsciously. In his blog, "The High Price of Free Will," Dr. Robert M. Price says, "Neuroscience reveals that when we think we make a decision, it is actually the conscious awareness of that choice having been made just beforehand deeper in the physical brain. We are, in short, taking orders, playing a role in a play we did not author—and (maybe) with no author" (*Zarathrustra Speaks*, July 2018). Be that as it may, it seems that some decisions are made consciously.

Some decisions must be made so quickly you don't have time to think about it while others take longer. But perhaps neither results from free will, even though we can believe it does. People choose the options that favor the perceived benefits more than the burdens, even though unconsciously.

This process can be likened to an iceberg where most of it is submerged in the subconscious mind. The top must go where the bottom takes it. But the perceived benefits always must be presumed to outweigh the burdens in all decisions, even if unconsciously. These can include matters of the heart as well as the mind, or maybe also hormones. One extreme example is that of Nadya Suleman, the "Octo single mom" who had fourteen children, eight of them in one birth after she had six others, all by in vitro fertilization. Another example: An Army veteran adopted five children with Down Syndrome after her own daughter was born with the birth defect. And another: At his age of eighty, actor Bill Cosby was convicted of sexual crimes that he committed many years prior during his very popular and lucrative career. One more: President Richard Nixon won forty-nine states for his second term, but he was forced to resign after he was threatened with impeachment for obstruction of justice.

Consider the decision to speed up to get through the caution light before it turns red and risk getting a ticket, or to come to a screeching stop and risk getting tail-ended. A baseball batter facing a ninety-miles-per-hour fastball has 0.45 second to decide to swing and to complete that action, but the fans in the stands can take their time deciding to be there. First, they must decide to go, then get a ticket, dress, and show up. Experiments show that once they become conscious, decisions seem to be controllable—fans could buy a ticket and decide not to go. But, is that really free will or predetermined by all the decisions that came before including invention of the game of baseball and construction of the stadium? The late, great boxing champion, Muhammad Ali, had an uncanny ability to avoid the attempted punches of his opponents and to retaliate instantly with deadly accuracy. But first, he had to decide to be a boxer and to train intensely, after his parents decided to birth him and their parents birthed them and so on back to the first parents.

Whether decisions are made consciously or not, decision makers all seem to assume the benefits are more valuable than the burdens involved. If this process is made conscious, it may be possible to make decisions with more confidence. American sage, Benjamin Franklin, explained his method of creating a decision balance sheet by drawing two columns on a sheet of paper and labeling them "for" and "against." He would list all the motives for any decision on each side and assign personal values to each one— say on a scale of ten—then he totaled up each side to make the best choice, after he subtracted the items of equal value on each side. However, Dr. Franklin also invoked the deity in the affairs of life, which seems to negate his rational approach to decision-making. He observed, "The longer I live, the more convincing proofs I see of this truth—that God governs in the affairs of men." Perhaps there are no decision mistakes, only predestined choices and inevitable consequences.

ABOUT THE AUTHOR

Lewis Tagliaferre has written more than one hundred magazine articles in the energy industry, published a technical journal for twenty-seven years, and written ten books on managing grief and the metaphysics of aging and facing the unknowns following death. Although he might be called a contrarian to established religious dogma, he prefers to be called a realistic mystic and explorer of the human psyche. An avid reader and researcher, his work is intended for those who are suffering loss and tragedy who find no comfort or security in traditional religious dogma. His books result from the necessity of surviving the untimely loss of his beloved wife at her age fifty-two from complications of breast cancer. The resulting shock and search for a belief system he could live with culminated in forming the principles of theofatalism. This belief is a spiritual pathway to serenity and contentment when your life is shaken and you realize it is God—generator, operator, destroyer—that is doing the shaking. Born in 1933 to immigrant parents, one German, one Italian, Tagliaferre grew up in Cumberland, Maryland, where he played trumpet and starred in drama and public speaking at Fort Hill High School (1951). He served in the US Air Force on a B-36 bomber crew during the Korean war (1951–1955). After attending college part-time for thirteen years earning degrees in electronics and business administration, he completed a long career in defense contracting and energy-related trade association management. He considers himself a recovered Baptist, deacon, and Sunday school teacher. His other books are titled: *Recovery from Loss, Kisses Aren't Contracts, Voices of Sedona, Baby Boomer Lamentations, Theofatalism, A Labyrinth Walk of Life, Creating Serenity in Chaos, Better Living, Better Dying,* and *The Bible You Don't Get in Church* (www.betterlivingbetterdying.com, www.amazon.com).

CPSIA information can be obtained
at www.ICGtesting.com
Printed in the USA
FFHW022049030919
54768296-60432FF